THE DEFEAT IN THE VICTORY:

An Interpretation and a Threnody.

Oh, how many wretched mothers and fathers were deprived of
their children! How many unhappy women were deprived of
their companions! In truth, my dear Benedetto, I do not believe
that ever since the world was created there has been witnessed
such lamentation and wailing of people accompanied by so great
terror. In truth, the human species in such a plight has need to
envy every other race of creatures; for though the eagle has
strength sufficient to subdue the other birds, they yet remain un-
conquered through the rapidity of their flight, and so the swal-
lows through their speed escape becoming the prey of the falcon,
and the dolphins also by their swift flight escape becoming the
prey of the whales and of the mighty leviathans; but for us
wretched mortals there avails not any flight.

Leonardo da Vinci.

BY THE SAME AUTHOR:

THE MENACE OF PEACE.

WOODROW WILSON AND THE WORLD'S PEACE.

GERMANISM AND THE AMERICAN CRUSADE.

THE GREATER WAR.

THE REVIVAL OF ITALY.

The Defeat in the Victory

George D. Herron

Simon Publications
2003

Library of Congress Card Number: 24016923

ISBN: 1-932512-03-9

Published by Simon Publications, Inc. P. O. Box 910455, San Diego, CA 92191-0455

These pages are inscribed to all who, deep in the
shadow of The Great Dissappointment, and
unable to see the ways they therein
take, still hopefully strive
for the redemption of
the nations

PREFACE

I.

NOT soon will there be an end of making many books about The War and about The Peace, even though the peoples be wearied of the matter and pray only to be delivered from the confusion of tongues and the army of apologists. Every new book seems either an impertinence or another turning of the sword in the nearly fatal wounds of mankind. Yet I am guilty of inscribing another book in the interminable catalogue. My book comes, timidly enough, with the excuse that it makes no pretence of conveying new information. It consists mainly of preachments, aspiring to no more than a possible dynamical value, and content if that be but momentary. Let me add this, however, that I am herein dealing with world-stuff my own hands have handled. What I say of The War and The Peace is a report of intimate contact with their invisible facts and forces.

To sum up the matter, these papers are the frank disclosure of a state of mind due to the perfidy of the Conference of Paris in general, and to the diplomatic defeat of President Wilson in particular. They are meant to be photographic of the present psychological plight of such as gave to Wilson's early gospel and leadership an active and even apostolic trust. The fact that these are entirely human documents, the reflex and refrain of profound disappointment and re-adjustment, and written in troubled hours snatched from futile, but, I hope, faithful services, accounts for their somewhat painful reiterations; for inconsistencies, also, which I would not conceal if I could. The relinquishments herein revealed, the conclusions rehearsed, the new promise rising from the wreck of the old, have all been reached hardly, and at great cost; and they will be better understood, I think, and perhaps more patiently considered, if I expose them upon the recurrent way I have come, and amidst the stern interrogations with which I have wrestled.

Of course, if merely my own state of mind were in question, it were not worth while that I have written or that anyone should read. I write because I express the serious mind of most European peoples about the great matter which is this book's concernment. It must be, too, that many in America are of the same mind, though assuredly the faith of other Americans was more moderate than mine, more rational indeed, and less propulsive and propagative.

I think I speak, moreover, for those who, whether they be American or European, neither wanted nor expected anything out of the war or the peace—who in truth neither wanted nor expected anything out of the world—except the privilege of serving with fidelity and to some purpose, and of seeing mankind started upon a nobler and happier history.

With one exception, "The Treason of France," these chapters were all written, as the reader will at once see, while Mr. Wilson was still President. Eight of the ten chapters have already been published in England (Cecil Palmer, London) under the title of "The Defeat in the Victory," and in Germany (Der Neue Geist Verlag, Leipzig) as "Die Niederlage im Sieg." Some of them, in whole or in part, have appeared as articles in European journals and reviews —in *La Semaine Littéraire*, of Geneva, *Gazette de Lausanne*, *The New Europe*, of London, *Das Tagebuch*, of Berlin, and in *The League of Nations*, an international review published in Bern by the Dutch-Swiss Bureau Pax. The substance of the first and last chapters has also been published in the series *Les Cahiers Idéalistes Français*, of Paris, in *The World Tomorrow*, of New York City, and as a brochure in Italy, in Switzerland, and in Germany. The second paper, "The Prometheus of Paris," appeared in *Le Monde Nouveau*, of Paris, together with a reply by Mr. William Morton Fullerton, and was previously given as an address before a gathering of university and literary men at the British Institute in Florence. "In the Light of the London Conference" was published in Mr. Ford's journal, *"The Dearborn Independent."*

The letters published in the Appendix will help the reader to an understanding of the opinions expressed in the chapters which precede them.

That an American edition of this book is so late in appearing is due to the fact that twice was the manuscript accepted for American publication, and twice suppressed suddenly and without explanation— once while the book was on the press. And it was only after a year's mysterious delay that I was able to get back the manuscript.

II

The above explanations are enough for the general reader, whom I would wish to pass immediately to the ensuing chapters. Yet there may be some who would be helped to an understanding of my contentions and predictions by some word as to their antecedency.

Until August, 1914, I had been a socialist and an antagonist of every form of militarism. I had never ceased from speaking against the government of nations by propertied interests; and against the maintenance of armies, either potential or in being, for the support of such government. But for some years, my hopes of a near time when each nation would become a true human commonwealth, and all nations advance together in mutual reverence and good-will, had been shaken by two facts—or what were facts to my apprehension.

The first of these was the purpose of Prussian Germany to impose her rule and her particular culture upon the world. I did not need to depend upon any French or British propaganda, or upon the testimony of any man, for a knowledge of what this Germany meant to do. I had been somewhat about the world, and had seen the Prussian purpose everywhere at work—in New York and London; in the middle of France and through the length of Italy; in Athens and Jerusalem; among Russian pilgrims from Odessa to the Jordan; from Cairo to the Soudan; down the pilgrimage road from Damascus to Mecca; in the educational institutions of England and America; in every sort of religious association in every country; in international socialist organization and activity. As long ago as 1908, in the pages of an English review, I had proclaimed the Prussian peril In the course of those pages, I had expressed the conviction that nothing short of a European social and political revolution could prevent war between Germany and England for a more or less planetary control. But, I confessed, since there was no sign of such revolution, and since therefore the world-changing war would inevitably come, all such as myself would be forced into choosing between the acceptance of a German order of things,—an order ultimately becoming universal,—and the support of military resistance on the part of the non-German nations; for the reason that, "if Prussia once gain the hegemony of Europe, the result will be a barbarian renaissance, followed by an abysmal human decadence."

The second fact standing over against my hopes was the absence of any hearty or honest preparation on the part of the German social democracy to prevent the foreboded war. The very quality of this fabled socialist party, as well as its pedigree and general perspective, was such as to reduce serious dependence upon it to a fatuous if not wilful credulity. The leaders had built up, it is true, an efficient and highly centralized organization; but the pattern thereof was Prussian, and they had inspired their followers with only a stolid mental serfhood. Neither in the socialist shepherds, nor in the multitudes they had trained to such repulsive docility, was any competent or largening thought of human life or society discoverable. It was but through partizan or sectarian eyes, through a sort of moral insobriety, that one could behold the probable end of war, or indeed any essential social transformation, in such action as German socialism was likely or able to take.

Moreover, no Junker professor was more complacent than the German socialist in assuming that the right ordering of the world lay in its Germanization. German superiority and authority were the very breath of the socialist spokesman's being. It was not that he deliberately thought it, but that he actually lived it. Every leader—Singer and Kautsky—the elder Liebknecht—even so noble a personality as Bebel—regarded other than German mankind condescendingly, and took the German transcendency for granted. The whole training and intellection of these, as well as their hierarchical habits and the servility of their followers, rendered any other than the condescending attitude toward the non-German world as impossible to them as it was impossible to the Prussian generals and teachers.

Yet, alas! the international socialist movement had taken the German authority at its own valuation; and had also indoctrinated itself with the materialist philosophy which the German made fundamental to socialist faith and propaganda. And from this fatality—this double fatality—came the fact that the socialist parties nowhere provided a higher political morality or public leadership than that provided by capitalist parties and the governing classes. From this fatality came also that pitiable impotence which made socialism an international shame and mockery in the day of The Great Catastrophe. It became obvious that the socialist movement itself, before it could either effect a new human order or prevent the wars inherent in the order now existing must be regenerated by a new philosophy and be compelled by a higher reason for being.

III

When the war came, and Wilson began to speak in the name of the American people, I was among

those who took him at his word. In his leadership, in
the principles he pronounced, loomed that better human
immediacy for which I had elsewhere vainly looked,
and without which I saw no reason for being alive.
Upon my faith in Wilson's fidelity to the faith he had
confessed, I built myself a new and pinnacled house
of hope for humanity. I can best expose my expectations by repeating some sentences from my little
book, "Woodrow Wilson and the World's Peace,"
published in the summer of 1917. "Woodrow Wilson
does not believe in war as a rational method of civilization. He does not believe in military might as a
continuing mode of justice or progress. He does not
believe that things are finally settled by war. He
sees war rather as a means of confusing old problems,
and of precipitating needless problems new. He con-
cedes to the strong nations no right to impose their
will upon the weak. He stands for a universal politic
so new, so revolutionary, so creative of a different
world than ours, that few have begun to glimpse his
vision or to comprehend his purpose. His eyes are
fixed upon a goal that is far beyond the present
faith of nations." "I perceive—or certainly seem to
perceive—that Wilson is not only the greatest states-
man that has appeared in the world for many years
—great indeed beyond comparison with any save
Lincoln: he is also a determined and tremendous radical: he is a redeemer of democracy. He is revolutionary beyond anything his contemporaries have
discerned." "Whenever and wherever the issue between property and the people has been clear, in not
a single instance has he stood for property, but in
every instance for the people" In the Federal Reserve
Banks as well as in other legislative achievements,
he has knowingly undermined certain of the foundations upon which our capitalist society rests; at the
same time he has been preparing foundations for a
truly co-operative society. Without proclamation,
with none of the jargon common to radicals, he has
shown himself more profoundly conscious of the

working-class than many of the working-class leaders; and this notwithstanding his previous academic career and associations. As compared with Wilson, there are socialist spokesman who are bourbon in their understanding and sympathy. As contrasted with America's President, the parliamentary leaders of German socialism are medieval reactionaries." "Wilson believes in the whole length and logic of democracy—democracy in things intellectual and spiritual. If we could look deep into this man's soul, I think we should find there the ideal of a world at last arriving at a universal communism of production and distribution, with a common and unfettered freedom as regards the right of each individual to choose the way in which he shall go, and grow, and give himself." "He believes that the Sermon on the Mount is the ultimate constitution of mankind; and he intends, by hook or crook if you will, by the wisdom of the serpent and the secrecy of the priest, to get this foundation underneath the unaware American nation. He cunningly hopes, he divinely schemes, to bring it about that America, awake at last to her national selfhood and calling, shall become as a colossal Christian apostle, shepherding the world into the kingdom of God."

Such was the faith I had not only held, but which I eagerly, even militantly, set about communicating to European peoples—both before and after America had entered the war. And until the President drew back before the two appeals appended to these chapters, I did not doubt the war would issue in a world delivered from many ancient wrongs, in a democratic redemption and federation of the nations, and in a high and happy transmutation of the whole relational life of man.

As I said in the beginning, it is in the defeat upon defeat of this faith, in the sorrow of its lost labor and battle, in the betrayals and disappointments so darkly visited upon it, in the shame of its dishonored pledges to the peoples, that my book has its source and compulsion. But, withal, heavy-hearted and red-

writ as its pages are, I yet dare to think them charged
with the self-same faith, resurgent and adventuring
itself anew, again militant and onward, again apostolic and communicable, and fixed again upon the
effectibility of the Christly world-order.

G. D. H.

CONTENTS

I.

THE PEACE OF PARIS: ALSO AN APOLOGY.

I have signed the Peace Treaty, not because I consider it a satisfactory document, but because it is imperatively necessary to close the war; because the world needs peace above all, and nothing could be more fatal than the continuance of the state of suspense between war and peace. The six months since the armistice was signed have perhaps been as upsetting, unsettling, and ruinous to Europe as the previous four years of war. I look upon the Peace Treaty as the close of these two chapters of war and armistice, and only on that ground do I agree to it.

. . . . . .

The promise of the new life, the victory of the great human ideals, for which the peoples have shed their blood and their treasure without stint, the fulfilment of their aspirations towards a new international order, and a fairer, better world, are not written in this Treaty, and will not be written in treaties. Not in this Mountain, nor in Jerusalem, but in spirit and in truth, as the Great Master said, must the foundations of the new order be laid. A new heart must be given, not only to our enemies but also to us; a contrite spirit for the woes which have overwhelmed the world; a spirit of pity, mercy, and forgiveness for the sins and wrongs which we have suffered. A new spirit of generosity and humanity, born in the hearts of the peoples in this great hour of common suffering and sorrow, can alone heal the wounds which have been inflicted on the body of Christendom.

And this new spirit among the peoples will be the solvent for the problems which the statesmen have found too hard at the Conference.

GENERAL JAN SMUTS.

It is true that with the war still so fresh, with its wounds still bleeding, one hears in authoritative circles cynical contempt for those ideals. The Government, when stripped of cant and hypocrisy, says, in effect, as exemplified by its acts: We did not fight for the rights of Belgium, or for the freedom of small nationalities, or the sanctity of treaties; talk of this sort is only fit for children, and we are practical people, we are Imperial thinkers. We fought for our own right hand, and we downed Germany because the trade rivalry between us had endangered our position; and now having made use of the banners that attracted to our side all that was good and generous and noble, we refuse to honour the draft that we have drawn upon humanity; not the military Imperialism of Germany, but our own military Imperialism prevails; in that sign we conquer the world; we rule by might, not right; and the spoils are ours, Profiteers, O Profiteers!

COLONEL ARTHUR LYNCH.

I.

THE PEACE OF PARIS: ALSO
AN APOLOGY.

I

WHEN the war came on, sweeping the nations into hell and wrecking the soul of man, it was as if an actual but insane Lucifer, outwitting God and capturing the power, had laid maniacal compulsion upon our humanity. Yet we assured ourselves his time would be brief. Catastrophe so complete, so inclusive; so destructive of all that both nature and man had dearly achieved; so full of every manner of torture and death and derangement; so consuming life's inner substance as well as its outer form;—such catastrophe must, we were certain, carry in itself its own early extinction: it would soon exhaust the power of the nations to continue it. So we counted the weeks till the war's conclusion.

But the weeks grew into years of incalculable moral and material ruin. The miles and millions of the dead increased till we ceased to number them—till death seemed all that really lived. As we brooded over it all, trying to understand, hunting for hands able to keep the world from the pit and finding none, our anguish not only obsessed our souls and our speech, often excluding all else: it became so encompassing that the uprooted hills, the crazed waters and the shattered air, all seemed to share it. Yet it was a helpless anguish, ignorant and uncreating: it provided no healing for the wounded and dying nations: it held neither solution nor constraint for a world organized for murder. The murder marched on, multiplying its hosts, the woes that waited upon it multiplying also, until at last the power to think and the power to pity broke down. The will to kill or to let die had become so absorbing, the infidelity of nation to nation and of man to man so commonly accredited, the protesting sympathies of both societies and individuals so impotent, that the whole expanding horror, eating into the very soul of things as its circles widened, mocked the mind's efforts either to penetrate or to reach round it. The mental apparatus and the emotional machinery were left without motivation—with neither achievment nor hope to keep them going. Imagination, its divine occupation derided, unable to purchase any good thing with its ancient wage, refused to work: and the heart, exhausted from long overfeeling, benumbed by the futility of its ablest promptings, finally ceased to feel. Without the strange apathy which came narcotically upon the nations, the hearts and the minds of many had not endured.

Whence it seemed, as year by year the world the redder and more reasonless grew, that the ends of all evil were upon us. There could not be more of evil, we said, than what we had seen and done—than what we were seeing and doing. It might even be that we were workers and witnesses of the world's awful end. The total catastrophe indeed appeared, betimes, to pronounce the conclusion of the human experiment, its failure too sustained and too irreparable, too prolonged and too costly to heaven, for further toleration. It looked as if God had had enough of the base and bloody absurdity of man.

II

Yet, potentially, a worse evil has come upon us. The Peace of Paris, were there no redemption from it, would prove a more infernal fall of **man, a more** desperate derangement, than the war. The treaties therein set forth, greedy and savage and lawless, overladen with dishonesties and evil complexities, and as crass as they are cruel, as ignorant and ravenous **and silly as** they are shameless, investing primitive revenge with capitalist modernity and epitomizing the capitalist culmination at its worst, are the shabbiest dissemblances that shabby minds ever essayed to impose upon or between nations. These are not peace, —these treaties of Paris: they are rather a pitiless provision for a military and predatory government of the world. They are pregnant with wars more destructive, both physically and spiritually, than history has yet registered, with the resultant prospect of a generation if not a century of Tatarean tortures for the whole family of man. Indeed, issuing from the betrayal of the faith of the peoples by the Conference, the times of universal terror and dementia are already setting in. Even the law of self-preservation has broken down,—desperately supplanted by the feeling that death, whatever it brings, is preferable to citizenship in the sort of world the peacemakers have provided.

III

But it is more than its early promise to the peoples which the Conference has betrayed. That were treason enough, surely, dissipating as it did the immeasurable spiritual treasure which both groups of peoples had heaped upon the Peace Table, besides quenching the hopes and ashing the altar fires of two thousand years. But what has been wrought, beyond all this, is the destruction of the indispensable basis of peace —the confidence of the peoples in each other. Out of their common cry for a mutual and federating understanding, out of their yearning for unity and fellowship, the Conference has created a world of division and contradiction, and has ensphered it in poisonous suspicion. No nation now trusts a present ally more than a former foe: mutual and hateful unbelief in one another prevails among all the tribes of men.

Even the desire for high renunciation and concordant action is vanishing. The peoples are no longer mooded, as they erstwhile were, for international comity and kindness; for a world confederate in a common good-will. The great body of conciliatory expectancy which had grown up about the principles enunciated by Mr. Wilson—and which principles the Conference professed as its reason for being—has by this same Conference been wounded to its death. No nation now believes in the utility of the ideal, in the actuability of collective righteousness, or in international brotherhood as a near possibility.

Furthermore, the Conference has destroyed what remained of popular faith in existing social control or political authority. By the wanton ignorance of their diplomacy, by their unbelief in the peoples, by the secrecy and cynicism of their procedure, the peace-makers have demonstrated the stark incompetence of the mere political mind for national or international interpretation and administration. They have equipped and universalized the feeling, already widely abroad, that the powers of government, as these are now constituted, are not only inadequate, not only partial to the powerful few, but parasitic and archaic as well, able to function only what is worst and defeat what is best in human relations and aspirations. If you get close to the peoples, you will find that they consider that Paris has let the secret out: they are awakening, they ominously believe, from the long hypnosis, the ancient spell, whereby the sheer might of possession has been able, in its own predacious interests, to govern and guide the human procession.

IV

Yes, whether it be for good or for evil, whether the fact be justified or baseless, it is undeniable that, as a result of the Conference, belief in the fraudulency and incompetence of current social and governmental organization is now generally and irrevocably active. Moreover, alas! though the faith in the old world has gone, no uniting faith sufficient for the effecting of the new has yet appeared. And no uniting faith can arise in man at the present low level whereon the

Conference has left him. Without some great spiritual influx, generating mankind anew, no salvation is near.

For the last and worst achievement of Paris is the debasement of mankind in its own estimation. When men consider their capacity for collective honesty and decency in the light of the Conference, the sense of humanity as trustworthy or important, the reverence of one human group for another, vanishes in mutual and helpless self-loathing, if not in laughter that is at once piteous and perilous. No other historic assemblage, no other congeries of events, has rendered human life so discreditable in its own eyes—has made man and his covenants so contemptible to himself. And his value daily lowers: man refuses to take shares in his own future. The word of a man, the word of a nation, has ceased to be coin in the human realm.

V

Yet the peoples expected a world of fraternal peace, at least in outline, to issue from the deilberations and decisions of the Conference. They had faith, before the Conference killed it, that such a world was effectible. They were ready to go the whole way that led to it. But the business which the assembled mighty ones took upon themselves was that of preventing this effectuation. And this defeat of the world's desire was made easy—was indeed made inevitable—by the fact that the peoples were not really represented at Paris; they had no actual voice in the Conference. The official representatives, self-appointed or named by each other, had no contact with the real will or wish of their respective nations; nor had they the mental tendencies or the moral experience wherewith to make the contact. The peoples were as sheep without shepherds; for they who made themselves the official shepherds proved, when all was said and done, as men who either served the Ancient Appetites or knew not what they did or whither they went.

*If he who was the Promethean exception to this characterization—if the one man to whom all the world then turned, upon whom the peoples waited as men had never waited upon man, had trusted them with the trust wherewith they trusted him, if he had only taken them into his confidence and openly appealed to them, if he had but accepted the divine challenge to rise to his appointed stature, he could have swung the world into a light that had never shone upon mortal policies and proceedings. Not since the sorry tale of man began to be told, has such power for good, for universal change upward, been in the hands of the single mere man. And history presents no mortal tragedy comparable to the failure of this man to capitalize,—diplomatically and spiritually and at its full value,—the power so confidently and universally thrust upon him. Nor is the tragedy lessened by the fact—if **we agree** that it is a fact—that the fatal causes lay more in the men that failed him and the forces that fought against him than within himself. Neither is it lessened if we admit, if we even brutally declare, as well we may admit and declare, that not Woodrow Wilson, nor all the political prophets, from Moses to Mazzini, had been wholly equal to the stupendous total of hypocrisy and treachery which conventionalized the proceedings of the Conference, and which made its last days a derision to gods, men and devils. Nor does the admission cancel the result that now the peoples, despairing and blackly distrustful, and the earth bitter with their tears, go leaderless and leaden-footed into the uncharted darkness.*

VI

But why did Paris fail—fail so easily and so utterly—in the face of an expectation so prevalent, so highly compulsory, as seemingly to render some divine fulfilment inevitable?

The failure lies in this, that the Conference, from its first morning until the drivelling later hours of its calamitous career, was under the control, occult but conclusive, of Europe's hoary masters—the money-lenders. It is these, their immemorial calling regarding not the souls of nations, and the weapons and the hostages of the world in their hands, who darkly prevailed at the Peace Table.

It was inevitable, therefore, that no spiritual principle should be given occupation at that Board. The influences there operative rendered the peace-makers infidel, from first to last, to the initial pledge and the professed creed whereon they came together. The Conference, blinding the eyes of its greatest participant and of his closest friend, devolved itself into a solemn meeting for the division of the spoils; for the allotment of fertile fields to the concessionaires. The incredible contrivances brought forward under the name of peace were born of either bargain or essential blackmail. Not the souls of men, nor the souls of nations, but oil and iron, coal and gold, potash and copper, turned the scales of decision. All the blood and tears of these terrible yet expectant years, all the assembled hopes of the beaten generations of men, were sacrificed by the Great Powers to the mighty usurers. The peace is theirs, the usurers' and the concessionnaires'—a peace whereby, through the highly-phrased diplomatic pimpery of their procurers, they filched the natural resources of the planet, and sentenced its populations to choose between national slaveries, death by starvation, and suicidal revolt. General Smuts was right about the Conference—and he but scantly hinted at his opinion of it—nothing could conceivably be as bad for the world as its continuance.

VII

But the condemnation is retroactive—gathering into its judgments others than the great ones directly responsible for the Peace. There are some who, though standing against the things done in Paris, and for the things left undone, yet feel heavily accountable. With such, though among the least, I belong—with them reduced to anguishing interrogation, and possibly to depthless remorse. I used all the small

influences I could mobilize for bringing America into
the war. Before that I had somewhat participated,
chiefly through friends, in preparing Italy to march
with the Allies. Nor does it matter that my words
and efforts counted for little, or if they counted for
nothing at all: I am as responsible as if I had contrib-
uted considerably to the Italian and American decisions for war.

I believed then—as I still believe—that the thing
we call Germanism incarnated the evil forces of
history, and conceived the assault which Germany
made upon humanity as their culmination. A German
world, as German was then minded, would have been
a world in which the soul of man had ceased to exist:
men would have become automata—things for the
creation of things. It was better that our history
should be wound up, that human life upon this planet
should cease, than that the world which Germany
then purposed should come into being.

But there was a greater reason—a reason reaching
beyond the mere military defeat of Germanism. I
believed profoundly, indeed religiously, that America's participation in the war would so transmute its
whole motivity and conclusion as to render it the
last great war, and furthermore, compel its ultimation
in a world-society of free and uplifted nations. I
knew the spirit of the young men of the great American Middle West: these believed themselves taking
up arms to set a host of wrong things right, to clean
up the world, and to make another such war impossible. The spirit of the first Crusaders was actually theirs, and they commonly came to Europe with
a high consecration upon them.

VIII

Yet another responsibility is mine. During the
months after America had entered the war, divers
highly-placed Germans came knocking at my doors
at Geneva, seeking to learn the mind of America
about their conduct and country, and hoping for some

word that would indicate a way of negotiation through American intervention. Although these came partly through my friendship with such men as Professors Foerster and Jaffe and Dr. Muehlon, they were chiefly inspired by the legend that I spoke the secret mind of the President—between whom and myself no word had yet passed. But the legend— growing out of my earlier defence of America and the President in the European press—produced for me a somewhat unique opportunity for observing the workings of the German mind, and for watching and reporting the developing European situation. I also took it upon myself to try to put what we Americans call "the fear of God!" into the German heart— to convince my German pilgrims that America meant war, and meant it to the overthrow of Germany.

That was in the earlier days of these pilgrimages. Later—and this is what so sternly concerns me now —I made those Germans really believe, as I myself really believed, that the Fourteen Points would be precisely applied, both as regarded Germany and as regarded Europe. Those whom I convinced thence convinced others of their countrymen. And this belief in the President's pronouncements as the assured and sovereign basis of peace, and in himself as their undefeatable and indeed providential guar- antor—this belief, promulgated from other points of vantage as well as my own, came at last to per- meate the German people.

Finally, it was this faith of the German people in the Fourteen Points and their author that wrought the defeat of the German armies in 1918. I would not subtract an iota from the glory commonly given unto France's great soldier—a glory which France has fully capitalized. But, if the truth be told, it was the word of Woodrow Wilson that, inwardly overthrow- ing the German Empire, prepared the victory which ac- crued to the sword of Marshal Foch. Moreover, by the time the Armistice was signed, the moral lordship of Wilson was supreme among the German tribes—if we accept the older and smaller Prussia. There was a fortnight wherein our President could have done with Germany what he would. If he had gone among them, nine-tenths of the German peoples would have asked only to have him say what they should do. It was in the power of the allies at that time, if not in the power of America alone, to have crowned the military victory with a new and spiritual motivation, with an actual democratic initiation, of the German Empire. That we did not do so is one of the war's several tremendous tragedies of lost and irrecoverable opportunity.

IX

Nor was it only Germany that waited—waited more than they that wait for the morning—for salvation at our hands. The Austrians hailed with joy the expected "Wilson Peace," and prayed for an American occupation and administration of their country. And though her sins were ancient and great and many, Austria was yet the seat of a people intellectually fair and fruitful, and precious to the future family of nations. Yet, behold! at first wantonly encouraged by the Entente and afterwards as wantonly abandoned, Austria today lies listlessly and tearlessly dying, too starved and too spent to care any more, bartering her beautiful garments to vulturous hordes for a last loaf of bread, and civilization made the poorer by her madly wrought miserable end.

And the Bulgarians,—who were far from being vanquished,—laid down their arms because they were persuaded that "the Wilson way" would be followed by the peace-makers. "Now that we have heard of the peace Wilson proposes," cried the Bulgarian soldiers to their officers, "we have no need to fight more: we will not fight more: we will not fight America: if you do not ask for peace on the day we have named, we shall march upon Sofia and from there make peace ourselves."

X

But lo! out of Paris has come the negation of all we confidently expected as the war's end and justification. Instead of the establishment of open or democratic diplomacy, diplomatic secrecy has been malignly and a hundred-fold multiplied. Where one secret treaty existed in 1914, scores of secret arrangements and understandings exist today—and not one of them to be relied upon overnight. If there were instances of international honor before 1914, there are none now. These three Old World continents are one monstrous weave of basest diplomatic duplicity and barter, network crossing network, and whole peoples daily sold back and forth for a farthing of advantage.

But even our first purpose in the war—that is, the military defeat of Germany—is far from fulfilment. I am not sure but that we shall see, two or three years hence if not sooner, that the victory belongs to a former and unredeemed Germany. The peacemakers have given it to her—not directly, but indirectly and more certainly—through the kind of treaties they have contrived.

It is a Prussian peace and worse, that Paris has imposed upon the world—a peace dependent upon military force—a peace that can only be maintained through converting Europe into a perpetual barracks. Not one settlement makes for else than corrupting intrigue and exterminative war. And, in the midst of the armed camp which Europe now is, Germanism is increasingly having its way. The Prussian masters, perceiving the woe the Conference has loosened upon Europe, and rejoicing in the international dementia as their opportunity, are preparing their new time. Without an interior revolution, or without some extraordinary intervention, the former Germany, riding the reaction against the international anarchy which Paris has generated, will come back into power, reorganizing Europe and dividing Asia with Japan— or mayhap with a militarized China.

Yet this is the lesser of the German evils coming out of Paris. The incalculably greater evil is the triumph of the former German mind over the world that fought the German armies. Granting we have defeated Germany militarily, Germany has conquered us morally. Our respective states, or those who govern them, have out-Prussianed Prussia in putting her political philosophy into practice. Indeed it would seem as if the nations which were at war with Germany have descended into a deeper hell than that whence she emerged against them, so completely has she captured their mentality, so utterly overthrown whatever formerly obtained among them of truth or scruple of decency in public information, declaration or debate. With the result that, when judged by the light that shone upon our planet from Woodrow Wilson's first interpretation and motivation of the war, our humanity has never so failed to keep faith with itself, has never sunk so below the level of its knowledge of the right, as its common condition today implies.

XII

Such is the work of the men who, with tremendous flaunting of cosmoginal banners, assembled themselves in Paris to make a new world. It is indeed a new world they have brought about—but with what quality of newness! No envy will ever follow them; neither, let us pray, will any emulation. The Conference,—a tawdry and tedious thing always, its reactions divided between boorish levity and abominable brutality, its speech and its actions destitute of even a suggestion of either spiritual or intellectual dignity in its supreme moments—has assured for itself a lamentable place in history: it was the creation of darkness, it sat and wrought in darkness, and it is darkness and the works of darkness that have proceeded from its portals upon the peoples.

XIII

But, though the peace-makers precipitated the darkness, and by them comes the deep fall of man therein, not unto them belongs the first and the only guilt: we who converted our pacifist convictions into petitions to our respective countries to wage war—to wage war against Germany and for democracy—to wage war against war and for the society of nations—we bear a well-nigh insupportable burden of accountability. We are answerable to our day and to the human future, we are answerable to God and to our accusing souls, for that veritable tragedy of the heavens, which the Conference of Paris has enacted.

XIV

I speak of the Peace of Paris, not of Versailles, because it is to Paris the black honor belongs. And the triumphal dragging of the delegates to Versailles, in order there to set off to French advantage the German shame, was as irrational and ill-mannered as it was vindictive and theatrical. In only one sense was Versailles appropriate: it afforded a fit stage for the apt display of the minds that contrived the treaty.

Yet it was the one place Frenchmen should pray heaven to forget. One must search the records long if haply and scarcely he find any good thing coming out of Versailles. Here is the seat of the most repulsive phases of French history—royal littleness, detestable intrigues, historic debaucheries, and the prodigious vulgarity of the Prussian crowning of the first Emperor of modern Germany. Yet from the Prussians —from their ostentatious humiliation of a defeated people—M. Clemenceau took his cue, outdoing them in the boast of his speech and the meanness of his manners.

It is a curious indication of the indecency of the public mind of our times that the signing of the Peace at Versailles produced no shock. One would have expected that the moral sense of mankind would revolt at the choice—especially against all that occurred in the infamous hour of the presentation and the signing. It is no exaggeration to declare that the summoning of the Germans to Versailles, along with the speech that accompanied the presentation of the Treaty, constitutes a crowning stupidity of modern diplomacy, and one of history's deepest disgraces. If the whole affair were a true index of man's spiritual capacity, if this were the best that man could do upon supreme occasion—especially after the seed of Christ had been in the human soil for two thousand years—then one indeed might well pray for the proverbial comet to end the human fiasco.

What a stupendous opportunity for a divine gesture, for a really redemptive quality of action, for spiritual majesty and messianic magnanimity, was thus so stolidly, so loutishly, thrown away! One can but marvel at the apparent insensibility of the peoples to this boorish debauchery of man's mightiest opportunity to justify his existence, and to bring order to his anarch-world. Imagine—had some place of noble memory been chosen; had Jan Smuts been appointed to hand the treaty to the Germans, and Wilhelm Muehlon or Friedrich Foerster been appointed by the Germans to receive it: then some word might have been spoken that would have prevented the black hypnosis now so heavy upon the soul of the world.

XV

Finally, it may aptly be asked of the writer, as it has been asked of the infinitely more significant General Smuts: "Why then, estimating the Treaty as you do, did you join with others, when it was presented to the Senate by the President, in appealing for its ratification?" The question is painfully pertinent. The inconsistency is glaring and beyond dispute—if one be held to a logical course of conduct. The answer, whether wise or foolish, is in the fact that the idea of the Society of Nations, even though poorly embodied, at that time seemed the one immediate hope of the peoples.

I would not choose a raft as a permanent habitation, as a safe and happy mode of traversing the seas. But if the ship had gone down and there were naught else to cling to, I would stay with the raft in the hope of riding it to safety. So I clung to the Covenant, appealing for its acceptance, because it seemed to afford the sole possible escape of the peoples from catastrophe worse than the war—worse than even the Peace. I had no thought that the Treaty would ever be executed: I looked upon the Covenant as but provisional at best—as indeed but an extension of the Entente Foreign Offices. But I did hope, as others hoped, that we might take the paradoxical course of accepting the Covenant in principle, to that end legally ratifying the Treaty provisionally, while at the same time, as a people, pronouncing our abhorrence of the Peace of Versailles as a whole and rejecting it morally. And I also conceived it possible that, once the League were created, even by its enemies, and however perversely embodied, the peoples would finally see to its democratic reconstruction and effectual empowerment.

Moreover, if America had come into the League, she would have dominated it—and that without regard to her numerical representation. And she would have dominated it spiritually—or morally if you prefer —and not merely because of her material and potential military superiority. In the presence of America, France would have hesitated about the militarization of her African dominions; and from the forboded terrors of conscript black millions Europe might have been saved. In the presence of America, too, the hand of Great Britain had not so easily traced the frontiers of three continents according to her commercial advantage—taking their sources of wealth unto herself, and so largely annexing Asia and Africa to her Empire. The present rampant and unashamed capitalist imperialism of the Entente Powers is in no small degree a result of the absence of the restraining influence of America from the League and the Supreme Council.

Such is the explanation of the acknowledged inconsistency. It was the hope of an early democratic seizure of the League in the first place, and the hope of preventing the free course of the prepared imperialisms in the second place, that moved me—that moved numerous better and wiser men—to pray the American adoption of the Treaty and the Covenant. It may be that this course is inconceivable to men to whose opinions I defer and whose friendship I hold precious; and, indeed, my early plea for ratification may yet seem inconceivable and reprehensible to myself.

Let that be as it will. It no less remains true that the idea of the Society of Nations, of the universal solidarity and indivisibility of human interests, is the most potent force in the world to-day; and the most creative. Hence it still seems to me that to this idea we must hold—no matter how inadequately or falsely it first be formulated. If the idea—veritable treasure of the heavens that it is—comes to us in the very earthen pottery of the Paris Conference, let us not destroy the gift in our disgust with the vessel. Let us rather go on to find the forms, let us purify ourselves to write the Covenant, which shall yet be as the true ask of that brotherhood of free nations which the Great Idea predicates, which it shall yet procure.

For despite Paris, despite the Conference caricature of the League, the idea of a world society, held together in freedom and by the bonds of a common good-will—the only bonds finally powerful and permanent—is appealingly and pervasively with us. The Great Idea has captured and exalted the purpose of the peoples; and it will increase, it will run its course with the stars, until its final and inclusive realization in a world ensphered in the justice of love.

II.
THE PROMETHEUS OF PARIS.

The settlement of every question, whether of territory, or sovereignty, of economic arrangement, or of political relationship, upon the basis of the free acceptance of that settlement by the people immediately concerned, and not upon the basis of the material interest or advantage of any other nation or people which may desire a different settlement for the sake of its own exterior influence or mastery.

PRESIDENT WILSON.

> All this ere he uttered his message
> I knew; yet feel no dishonor
> In suffering wrong for a foe.
> Ay, let the lightning be launched
> With curled and forked flame
> On my head; let the air confounded
> Shudder with thunderous peals
> And convulsion of raging winds;
> Let tempests beat on the earth
> Till her rooted foundations tremble;
> The boisterous surge of the sea
> Leap up to mingle its crest
> With the stars eclipsed in their orbs;
> Let the whirling blasts of Necessity
> Seize on my body and hurl it
> Down to the darkness of Tartarus,—
> Yet all he shall not destroy me!

THE PROMETHEUS OF AESCHYLUS.

The first real, earnest religious faith that shall arise upon the ruins of the old worn-out creeds, will transform the whole of our actual social organization, because every strong and earnest faith tends to apply itself to every branch of human activity; because in every epoch of its existence the *earth* has ever tended to conform itself to the heaven in which it then believed; and because the whole history of humanity is but the repetition—in form and degree varying according to the diversity of the times—of the words of the Dominical Christian Prayer: Thy Kingdom come on Earth as it is in Heaven.

JOSEPH MAZZINI.

II

THE PROMETHEUS OF PARIS

I

IN the late autumn of 1918, a revered and venerable executive of the International Red Cross went from Geneva to Vienna with such scant supplies as he could hastily gather for the children's hospitals, at that time destitute of medicines and food, and without even rags wherein to wrap their piteous patients. In one of these, to some hundreds of children whose bodies had become as mere stricken shadows, the good man was one day sorrowfully explaining his inability to provide them with some meagre festival for the Christmas soon approaching. "O! but it doesn't matter," exclaimed certain of the children, "Wilson is coming, and everything will be right." They had talked it over among themselves, there in that helpless hall of mercy, and these little victims of the lust of power, starved as they were, and withering away, were together caught up in a marvellous expectancy. The coming of Wilson became to them the approach of a providential presence. It was as if a heavenly king, bringing his kingdom with him, were about to displace not only their own familiar misery, but the earth's round war and want as well, making it a place of peace, plenty and joy for all who dwelt upon it. Nothing would have seemed to these children so incredible, so shocking and profane indeed, as that anyone should doubt. Wilson was coming: soon all would be well—well with themselves, well with the world.

So it universally seemed, for a while. The trust of the *Innocenti* of Vienna ran unitingly from nation to nation, till the coming of Wilson took on the general aspect of a divine and redemptive appointment. The portents of his power, mighty to accomplish its messianic ends, seemed writ on all horizons; and the world's tough heart, so experienced and old, grew young and glad with anticipation. It was all but for a moment, it is true, but it was the moment of man's ablest and most peremptory possibility. Not before had the centuries set before the peoples, not before had they set before a single man, such importuning doors of predestinative opportunity.

Yet the world closed its doors upon the man: the man closed his doors upon the world: the opportunity and the man have gone by: and thus are we witnesses and partakers of a tragedy of unparalleled proportions. Whence came the tragedy, and what are its ultimate issues—such is the theme of this paper.

II

My theme leads straightway to Paris. For the question of Paris, when the delegates took their seats, was the question of Wilson. The to-be or not-to-be of Wilson was identical with the to-be or not-to-be of the promised new ordering of the world. The hopes of the nations all centered in him. It was he, Woodrow Wilson, who was to make all things new: it was he who was to enable the democarcy that had so long failed: it was even he who was to prepare the way of the earth-peace of the Christ.

And if Wilson had there stood precisely by the principles he had proclaimed, neither abating nor compromising one jot or title; if he had gone the whole way he had projected for himself, turning neither to the right hand nor to the left; then the universal expectation might have been somewhat fulfilled: the tribes and the nations would have all gathered around him, nor mortal government had been able to stand against him.

But nothing less than the whole way would have answered—better eleven-tenths than less than ten-tenths. Even had he gone nine-tenths of the way, and failed of the last tenth, the world and he would have been no less lost than they are now. Yet neither he nor the Conference took the first step: the way was not even entered upon: and thus it is that we—we and our institutions everyone—have gone down into the inscrutable times and tortures of our present hell.

Yes, if in Paris Wilson had stood, he could have conquered the world for his Idea. He did not stand: he stooped: and the world and he were lost. And since in Paris he did not stand, if in Washington he had but stooped, he could then have achieved his own and the world's deliverance. But alas! just as he stooped where he should have stood, so he stood where he should have stopped. And the great deliverance, departing hence, abides beyond the present world's end

III

The beginning of the tragedy was the meeting-place of the Conference. The choice was fatal both to Wilson and to the principles he had pronounced. Under the circumstances of the year 1919, any city would have been more favorable than Paris to the Peace the world needed and expected. The city of light had become a city of darkness. The old and the real Paris of letters and arts, of intellectual selection and stimulation, had closed its doors against the hordes attendant upon the Conference. The Paris of the mandarin and the financier, the Paris that preys upon the body of France, had come aggressively into the open. The governing forces of this Paris were avarice and revenge— avarice converting revenge into economic advantage and political power.

From this Paris, also, the roads of international evil all radiated, and to this centre they all returned. All that was perverting and pestilential in diplomacy and finance had here its focal influences, its poisonous springs. To this one centre, and by this centre evoked, came the Old Appetites, receiving promises of concessions in exchange for the support of France required for the establishment of her military supremacy in Europe. Paris had indeed become the capitol of the world's worst forces; and all these were working to destroy the contractual principles, at once just and magnanimous and redemptive, which the Allies had solemnly signed with Germany.

I searched the quarters of the Conference again and again for one effectual impulse making for the healing of the nations. The Light which, though never without its witnesses in the world, had so singularly pierced the state-papers of Wilson, finding thence its moment of free play among the nations—that Light I thought haply to glimpse somewhere in Paris. Neither the Light nor any of the things I sought did I find—no, not one. But I found an atmosphere so foul that it laid paralysis upon the soul—even unto the soul's finest senses. It was an atmosphere penetrated by no spiritual oxygen—an atmosphere suggestive of the sulphur and brimstone of the pit—an atmosphere of horror I pray never to breathe again.

Night upon night, walking the dimmed streets, I sought relief from the peace-makers in the faces of the miserable; and betimes I watched these when the great ones, ensconced behind their armed charioteers, wheeled imposingly through the palace gates. It was more than curiosity, more than misery, I saw in those serried sullen faces and the eyes that peered out of them. It was the reserved but gathering doom of our civilization I there read—a civilization whose soul and whose qualities, despite all moral appearances and religious professions, to-day seems essentially of the jungle: a civilization which is the prowling place of every hissing and ravenous thing, of everything that creeps and deceives and devours: a civilization, in fine, fitly crowned by the Peace of Paris.

Among the thousands gathered there, in one interest and another; amidst the staged and garish movements of the great ones, with their stupendous yet impotent secrecies, their marked and impenetrable ignorance; amidst the swarming nursery diplomats with their self-conscious hurries and aperies, and bursting with their secrecies also; amidst the chariots of the diplomats and the generals, cleaving their ways through the ominous crowds; amidst the whole infernal pretence and frivolity, the total sham and strut and lie of things, one look-

ed in vain for any sign of the Son of Man: one had only
the recollection of the prediction He left upon Jerusalem,
ere He climbed the hill of His sacrifice. And it is with
no irreverence toward Him who spake as never man
spake that I say that Woodrow Wilson and his Table
of Principles had as little chance of acceptance in Paris
as had Christ and his gospel in the City of the Sadducees.

IV

Nor were the perils of the Conference within the walls
of Paris only: they proceeded from the whole of France.
The contract which she and her allies had signed with
Germany, France never intended to keep: she stood for
its violation from the start.

I wish not to be misunderstood by this statement. The
splendor of France through the war, as she breasted and
beat back the German hordes, is beyond praise. In her
military traditions, so centuried and so illustrious,
so replete with chivalrous and even saintly leaders
as well as with crusading armies—in these France is
peerless among the nations. But when this is said, let it
also be said that it was France which procured the defeat
of Wilson. Ere ever he departed from Washington, the
politico-financial group which governs France had deliberately and systematically sabotaged the President and
his program. Even before the armistice had been signed,
the agents of the French Government, in every part of
Europe and Asia and Africa, had faithfully carried out
their instructions to discredit Wilson, to undermine his
peace program, to bring derision upon his Society of
Nations. And this counter-activity, suicidal on the part
of France in the end, continued throughout Europe
during the life of the Conference.

Moreover, the dread of Wilson, and of American influence at the Peace-Table, had not tarried till victory
was at hand. Before America had entered the war, when
it still seemed that the Russia of the Czars would count
for the overthrow of Germany, France had warned her
Eastern Ally against the results of American participation. She had secretly asked the Czar's government to

discourage such participation on the ground that Wilson's presence would imperil the peace she and Russia then mutually contemplated—France upon the Rhine and the Czar in Constantinople.

V

France to-day complains of the position in which she finds herself. She views the present condition of Europe as due to her concessions to Wilson—concessions necessary to keep him in Paris, and to secure his consent to the triple compact which practically stigmatizes the League of Nations as an illusion. She would have made an altogether different peace, she says, had it not been for Wilson. And so she would: she would have carried her frontiers to the Rhine—and this in addition to her having multiplied by two if not three the actual cost of the damage done by the Germans.

Now that America has refused to guarantee the military domination of the Continent by France; now that America will not underwrite the indemnity which Germany has been forced to promise but can never pay; France grows daily more bitter against Wilson. All the official bathos about the eternal link of friendship between France and America does not in the least alter the stark truth that to-day Wilson stands in the French mind as an enemy co-equal with Germany.

In fine, the exact position in Paris is this: the French politico-financial governing group, having dominated the Conference and directed the deception and rejection of Wilson, and beholding now the perdition of Europe as a result, would place upon him the blame for its own base behaviour, would charge him with having wrought the ruin which is the work of its own sinister gestures, its own mercenary intrigues, and would finally make Wilson pay the cost of his own crucifixion.

VI

It is easy to understand the French state of mind. The terror of the German has been upon the Frenchman for two thousand years.   Since Julius Caesar, at the head of the Gauls, drove the German back across the Rhine, the horror of him—of his dishonorableness as well as his rapacity and savagery, has been in the blood of France, and her children have drunk the horror in the milk of their mothers.   Yet France has taken the one course to fix the German in his ancient ways, and to shut against him all doors to repentance and change.   The fear of the French people has been exploited by the French politico-financiers for their own base ends.   The world-ruin which the Prussian Junker began the diplomacy of France has carried on to completion.

The effect has been that France to-day stands alone. At the signing of the Armistice, she had the first place of honor among the nations—she was indeed the beloved of all peoples.   Her place no one begrudged her: it was by all freely accorded.   And, furthermore, no one disputed—and no one ought to have disputed—that in the Great Settlement, the first consideration must be given to France.   She had earned this consideration, and that she should have it was universally agreed upon as the first justice of the treaties to be negotiated.   But now, under the government of her mandarins, she has become suspect among the nations.   And the French people ought to know this: for it is not they, it is their governors, who have brought them to this evil pass, and made them believe evil to be good.   It is the governors of France, who, in achieving the ruin of Wilson and his hopes, have thereby achieved the dishonor if not the ultimate ruin of France.

VII

But beyond France, consequences as evil as the choice of Paris flowed from the President's failure to appreciate the primal opportunity of his own diplomacy—namely a working union of the Anglo-Saxon peoples. He doubtless saw the import and even the practicability of such a union—of at least a moral and economic federation.   Yet he practically proceeded without the support which the British people was then ready to give.

If England could have certainly depended upon essential union with America—though that union need not have been formal or written—she was prepared, I think, to follow Wilson at Paris. "If we can count upon Wilson," said England's most accomplished diplomat to the writer, "Wilson can count upon us to the last syllable." It is not going too far to say that England might have accepted America's mind about Ireland, and mayhap about Egypt and India, if she could have foreseen America surely entering a permanent Anglo-Saxon fellowship. And such a fellowship or federation would have been the surest foundation for a democratic world.

The accomplishment of this Anglo-Saxon federation was immeasurably more important than the sort of League of Nations that has issued from Paris. That England has now reverted to her ancient iniquitous diplomacy, that she is now covertly annexing another considerable portion of the planet to her Empire, is at least partly a result of the failure of Wilson, from whatever cause, to base his peace-program upon an all-Anglo-Saxon union: other foundation than this there was not.

VIII

Wilson being what he was, the Conference was not the place for his presence. He was here caught amidst diplomatic conventions to which he was wholly unaccustomed and for which he had no disposition. For the ancient psychology of these conventions, for the hypocrisies and duplicities that are the stuff of them, he was temperamentarily unprepared. He was no match for the evil marshalled against him—especially when he descended to fighting it upon its own terms. He had had no experience with it: he had no understanding of it: he had no weapons wherewith to cope with it. Nor had he at any time a real knowledge of what was going on, either in Paris or in Europe generally. He was ill-advised, on almost every question, by his meagre-minded counsellors—even when they were men of high desire, intent upon the creation of a new world-order. He was duped, as they were baffled, in most of the decisions reached, by the imposture of the diplomacy he had thought to set aside—the European diplomacy which, notwithstanding its staged and sounding traditions, is both impregnably ignorant and aboriginally unmoral. To speak coarsely but exactly, the successes of this diplomacy are of the moral order of the successes of the sneak-thief. Be its phrasing soever grandiloquent, be its garmenture soever grandiose, its actual achievements are the continuous cheat of liberty, the debauchery of the souls of nations, and the consequent inhibition of any real international morality.

IX

Nor was Wilson disarmed only by Europe's diplomacy: his situation was more subjective, more psychological than that: he underwent, from the first hour, a state of utter inner isolation. For he belonged to an entirely different world than that of the men with whom he had to do. He and they had no language wherewith really to communicate one with another. Even the semblances of contact and communion were farcical and pitiful.

Yet Wilson was immeasurably more than the Presbyterian dullard Mr. Keynes has portrayed. He knew the men with whom he had to do better than they knew him. He did not, it is true, discern when and how they entangled and deceived him; but he did discern their motivity—the ground and the goal of their action, while the ground and the goal of his action were to them unintelligible. To them he was like unto a man from a different planet, and he remained their unreadable riddle to the end. They thought, after a little, that they had taken his measure; and, under the assumption that his stature was altogether less than they had supposed, they practised upon him what history will finally decide to have been the Great Deception. But never mortals made a greater mistake. It was not Wilson's lesser measure they had taken; it was their own smallness of stature, their own meanness of mind, their own blindness to both the present and the future, their own political immorality and total inadequacy indeed, which they disclosed to an astonished and anguished world.

They prevailed, no less—gaining Wilson's signature to a treaty which not only overthrew himself and his principles, but which may prove to be the death-warrant of civilization. They brought about his immolation upon his Idea; they gave him the foul honor of a shadowy and false League of Nations in place of the World-Society he wanted, persuading him it was the best that could be had; they thought that, by sending him home shorn and dishonored, they had shaped his Idea into an instrument for the pre-emption and exploitation of the sources of the world's yet undeveloped wealth. But, though they fooled him so ruinously, they fooled themselves infinitely more—and all the world is taking knowledge of themselves and their folly. The democratic peoples are seeing to it that the Great Deception stands exposed; and history will tell a different tale from what the diplomats and the journalists tell now. Even to-day, the stature of Wilson, beshadowed as it is, still looms over the world, while the peace-makers of Paris go down beneath the contempt of peoples now living and of peoples to come.

X

But the President was also the victim of his own delegation. We cannot acquit Hotel Crillon of responsibility: it would be hypocrisy on our part, it would be unfair to Europe, to try to do so. It is true that America commanded the extraordinarily able and devoted services of Mr. Hoover and Professor Kellogg and their co-workers. But withal, the present bitterness of Europe against America is justly grounded, in part, upon the ineptitude of the Crillon. There was no coherent or uniting purpose operative within that house of immortally unhappy memory. The lack of candor there prevailing was as childish as it was woeful. The jostling attachés—each centered upon the amount of achievement he could get set down to his own credit—added a sordid absurdity to the general futility. All in all, it was an extraordinarily incompetent if not fatuous assemblage the Crillon contained—an assemblage quite unfitted to confound the old world and begin the new. And, mentally and morally constituted as it was, filled as it was with conflicting egotisms, some of them ludicrous enough indeed, the Crillon was quite the last place to obtain or to give the knowledge needed by the President or the American people.

The Crillon's continuous play of cross-purposes, the rivalries and concealments that set off the personal court of one Commissioner against another—these were constantly creating difficulties and disasters where none need have existed. For instance, on two different occasions the Adriatic question might have been settled —settled quietly and conclusively—had it not been for preventive interference in the American Commission to Negotiate Peace. A consequence of this interference was the injustice toward Italy which the President was misled into perpetrating. I have called this an instance, and such it is, for it stands not alone: it is but a single example of the disasters accruing to Europe through the ignorant and egotistic action of one or another individual connected with the American delegation.

XI

But the President cannot himself be acquitted of responsibility for the Crillon—for the continuous web of baffling circumstance in which he was thence caught. He did not know how to choose men, or how to adjust himself to the men he did choose. It is well to remember that Lincoln chose the greatest of the nation for his official associates. Nearly every member of his Cabinet had been his political opponent; and, at the time they were chosen, he was held in contempt by at least two of his ministers, besides his Secretary of State. Yet he knew how to co-ordinate these men and to make himself their master—for it is a quality of big men to recognize a master when they meet him. But only did Wilson not chose men of the right size,—always excepting the very able and honest but over-modest General Bliss,—but he was unable to use the men he did choose. This defeat of inability to work with others, to co-operate with men anywise his equals, must be candidly acknowledged.

XII.

Yet a hid but greater disaster to the President's cause lay in his early choice of the man he *could* work with—in his curious toleration of the regency of Colonel House, who served the imperialisms of England and France with such acceptable if blind fidelity, and at such ultimate cost to his own country; who so sagaciously increased himself proportionately to his master's decrease. The damage done to Wilson and his work by that regency is known only to the few; and even to these it remains inexplicable—inexplicable that so superior a mind as that of Wilson should for so long a time be guided by a mind so essentially inferior; inexplicable that such stupendous things as the President had to do with,—things that might well have broken the heart or wrecked the mind of a god,—should have been so largely in the presumptuous hands of this omnipresent but inconsequential friend.

Let it be said at once that neither the question of House's disinterestedness as regards humanity nor the question of his personal fidelity to the President enters into the disastrous matter. His good motives and amiable manners cannot repair the woeful issues of his assumption of managerial relations toward the President, toward the United States of America, toward the world in general.

From the beginning of Wilson's presidency, indeed, the influence of the lesser man over the greater was fatuous and fatal. For House was very far from being a Richelieu or a Cavour or a Seward. The things he told the President to do were generally things the diplomats wanted him to have the President do—and the diplomats were puppets of the money-lenders. As to the actual problems of the peoples, House knew little or nothing. What he took to be superior and intimate information was often a crass or childish misinformation.

Long before Paris, and more than Wilson has even been aware of, and for months before we had entered the war, Europe had accepted the regency of House, taking his voice as the voice of both the President and

America; taking his word as the substance of the things which Europe trusted America would provide or procure. Even in the recently published correspondence between Mr. Page and Mr. House, it is House who stands out as the one who counts: the President appears almost in the light of the youthful prodigy and House in the light of the patient impresario. But by the time Paris was reached, House had largely usurped the functions of both the President and the Secretary of State. It had come about that it was to House the diplomats and the missioners of Europe went, rather than to the President. It was House's word that was taken as either the word the President had spoken or would be caused to speak. And, indeed, the things House wanted the President to do, what he had told or would tell the President to do, what he had telephoned or telegraphed the President to do, fell too frequently and familiarly from his lips. And well had it been for the world if the President had ceased doing the things of House two years sooner than he did.

And the irony of it all is not diminished by the manner in which House came out of the catastrophe with praise of all men. When the storm broke upon the President, when we as people, drunken and debauched as never in our history, became as a mob of hounds, howling for the blood of our shattered and possibly dying chieftain; it was House who found shelter and sympathy in every camp—the camp of the super-capitalist and the camp of the arch-socialist; the camps of the British imperialist, the French Chauvinist, the New York bankers, as well as the camp of the intellectuals whose sympathies were with the Bolshevist; the camp of the President's worst foes as well as that of his few remaining friends. As regards the management of his personal place in the public mind, one must ascribe to House an especial genius. It is not every man that could win the sympathies of the American liberals who support *The New Republic* and at the same time congratulate and be congratulated by Monsieur Tardieu and his tribe. Jesus could not have done it—nor any of the apostles.

XIII.

And so, resulting both from his own mentality and that of the men about him, Wilson was lost in the thick darkness of Paris—a darkness enveloping the nations. Into that darkness he daily descended deeper: nor ever did he find his way out. He had a State Department that was never true to him, and to which he never confided his mind. Toward the last, when he listened at all, it was to little men, as futile as they were servile. Those who could and would have saved him, those who could and would have helped him save the world, found their influence cancelled by the inmates of the Crillon—who also increasingly cancelled the influence of each other.

Thus it came about that Woodrow Wilson at Paris was as effectually and densely walled in against the knowledge he needed, was as hermetically sealed against the truth, as was ever the Czar at the Winter Palace or the Kaiser among the courtiers of Potsdam. And that the truth came not near to Kaiser or Czar was relatively unimportant: for, after all, they were the creatures of the courts and the courts made the real decisions. But Wilson was his own master: and upon his relation to the truth—whether that relation be one of ignorance or knowledge—depended the course and the condition of our collective humanity for no one knows how many centuries.

XIV.

Because Wilson did not know the truth regarding the things with which he had to do, not one thing which he went to Paris for did he get. He wanted the Society of Nations: he got an instrument whereby British imperialism and French finance may exploit the world—and exploit it, very often, in covert co-operation with misguided or corrupted revolutionary movements. He believed the blockades ought to be lifted: he promised the writer of these words they should be lifted: he did not get them lifted. He knew that the Entente Powers had pledged Germany and Austria to make peace on the basis of the Fourteen Points: he watched these same

Entente Powers perjuring themselves without stint or shame: yet he failed to head the Conference toward honesty in either purpose or action. He had bespoken a peace that would make an end of war: he was tricked into signing a covenant of revenge and destruction—a peace emsphering the world in war indefinitely.

Finally, he no longer knew what he did in any particular. He strained at gnats and swallowed caravans of camels. Beguiled by the worst Balkanese politicians, he pivoted the peace of the world upon the town of Fiume —whilst England annexed empires, whilst France betrayed Armenia, whilst Japan took possession of the teeming populations and resources of the richest coast of China. Italy, the only country in Europe which supported Wilson in the beginning, and which would have stood by him unshakenly, if he had stood by his principles, he was misled into wantonly alienating. He was complacent about the creation of a Poland that is a monstrosity as well as a French military satrapy, and that will dissolve as a sand-castle the moment the Polish armies are starved into demobilization. He allowed peoples clamorous for the right of self-determination to convert that right into power to determine the destinies of other peoples than themselves—into the right to hold down alien populations by force of arms. And the conclusion of it all is his insistence—involving the sad insistence of those who followed him and for whom history will afford no redress such as it will afford him—upon the ratification of a peace which incarnates all the abominations he himself had condemned.

XV

Yet, paradoxically if you will, Woodrow Wilson was and is a curiously honest man. He came to Paris in all sincerity, with all high consecration upon him, fully purposing the realization of the international order he had previously proclaimed. There lives no man against whom the charge of hypocrisy is more groundless. The faults that brought about his defeat were mental faults —spiritual if you prefer—but they were not the faults of insincerity or deliberate deviation from the end he had in view.

Be it remembered, besides, that Wilson bore a burden compared with which the burden of Lincoln was local, and easy to be borne. Wilson had taken upon his shoulders—or let us say into his heart—a political pain and shame universal. He had undertaken to change the historic ways of the nations—to change the course which human policy had hitherto pursued. He was attempting, blindly but in all sincerity, to change men from creatures into creators; to persuade our humanity to take the course and the reins of its evolution into its own hands. And no mortal brain could bear that burden, no mortal heart could endure that strain, if the brain, if the heart, were unsocial and alone.

Moreover, as the result of persisting in the great undertaking alone, Wilson entered, at last, that worst wilderness of the soul—the wilderness of inner question and conflict. It was inevitable it should be so. The day following his first compromise required two compromises: the next day required four: the day after required eight: and so on, in geometric progression. In the end, after the diplomatic gambling was done, the devil had all the divine coin Wilson brought to Paris, and Wilson was left with naught but bewrecking delusions. And it is impossible that Wilson, whatever his psychology, should not now be questioning his course at Paris, and be passing through times of spiritual chaos as a consequence.

XVI.

Wilson should not have gone to Paris except uncompromisingly—except he were prepared to denounce the Conference, even to destroy it, the moment he found it false to its contractual principles: these principles constituted the only ground upon which it had any right to act. If, instead of presenting himself at the Peace-Table, he had sent the strongest body of men he could name, irrespective of party, it is probable, or at least possible, he would have retained the moral sovereignty he there lost: for his enemies would have had less occasion and advantage: it was his personal approach that bestirred them to prepare all things against him. But, having taken his seat, he should have arisen and departed therefrom the instant he discerned the direction the Conference was minded to pursue. Had he taken this first brave step, and thence appealed straightway to the peoples, not a government in the world could have stood against him—not even his own.

Or else, on discovering what Paris intended to do, he should have returned to Washington, taking his delegates with him, leaving Europe to make her own peace. Had he done even this, not a government in Europe would have lasted overnight—and the change would have been effected with little shedding of blood. The Europe of the peoples would have come to birth, and have come to Washington for peace according to Wilson's pattern.

But he chose neither course: he remained in Paris and became sport for his enemies. The result we know—a peace which has outraged the soul of the world —a peace which has delivered mankind to its devourers. Hence it is war which now possesses the world—war between nations; war between classes; war between religions; war between races; and, beneath and above all, war between rival financial groups for the economic hegemony of the planet.

XVII

Yet all this I say with a certain inner reservation and interrogation. Suppose Wilson foresaw, at least in part, the downfall of himself and his program as a result of his choosing to stay in Paris. Suppose he knowingly sacrificed his high place in the mind of Europe, and also the support and sympathy of his own country, for the negative result of preventing the complete triumph of the old world, or of at least compelling it to disclose itself nakedly to the peoples. Suppose, finally, he elected to undergo his destructive defeat in the belief that he could thereby—and only thereby—get his Idea of the Society of Nations into the world, and that, no matter how falsely shaped and clothed the Idea might awhile be, it would yet ultimately be potent to procure its own worthy embodiment.

There are those of us who would have had him take the opposite course: who would have had him act absolutely and not relatively—who indeed did our vain utmost to dissuade him from the course he did take and to persuade him to the course he did not take. Yet he may have been right and ourselves wrong. It may be that the generations will soon inscribe the matter in their ultimate annals.

For those of us who try to proceed absolutely instead of relatively have naught to set down upon our side of the argument. Our lives, so far as we are able to perceive them, are naught else than one changeless fool's errand, one continuous collision and futility. We are never able to adjust ourselves to the hateful facts of a world so surcharged as ours is with anointed lies and blood-lusts and rapine. We are never cured of our curious childhood and its helpless naiveté. We never conceive that the world will believe and speak and do the evil that it really does believe and speak and do. Whence we have nothing to show but failure added to failure. So it may be that ours are the wasted lives, the lost opportunities, and that our earthly careers count only in God's great scrapheap. So Joseph Mazzini thought —that the world had been right and himself wrong—as he lay dying, deserted and dishonored by his own Italy, in the lonely house of the woman of Pisa.

Hence I admit that it may be that Woodrow Wilson, in adding compromise to compromise, not only did the greater thing than such as the writer would have had him do, but that he made the greater sacrifice. It may be that, deliberately immolating himself upon his Idea, he became at once a victim and a bearer away of the political sins of humanity. If perchance this be so, then there is only one historic tragedy greater than his.

XVIII.

There is a lesser tragedy analogous to his—though the analogy be very limited. It is that of the dreamer of Luxemburg, Emperor Henry VII, coming over the Alps in 1310, accompanied by little more than his body-guard, to unite Italy and restore and sanctify the Roman Empire. He appeared trustfully in a European world that was but a hive of intrigue and assassination. "He was," as a great historian has said, "too honest for his age, and he did not realize the duplicity with which he had to deal." Especially was Henry's guileless honesty, the historian goes on to say, "unintelligible to the hard-headed business men of Florence."

But there were those who hailed his advent as if it were the coming of the Messiah to compose the world's conflicting actions and to establish the literal kingdom of heaven. Chief among these who went forth to meet him, as he came down the Mont-Cenis, was Dante. Kneeling to kiss Henry's feet, hailing him as the "Angel of the Lord" and the "Deliverer of the World," Dante believed the Emperor to be the one who was to fulfil his own ideal of the monarchy. While Henry was still upon the Alps, the poet addressed to the princes and governors of Italy an epistle wherein he exclaimed "Hosanna to thee, suffering Italy, now wilt thou be envied of all." "Let the oppressed rejoice, for their redemption draweth near. Let all who have endured injuries like unto mine forgive and grant pardon, for now the Shepherd that cometh from God will lead us back to the fold."

Yet, withal, in less than three years, Henry lay defeated and dying in the village of Buonconvento; and Dante's dream of the world as one Christian Roman Empire, with one Emperor as the executive of the world-state and one Pope as its spiritual shepherd, faded away for ever. Even the name and the romance of Henry have been forgotten by all save the historians and the lovers of Dante.

Woodrow Wilson is more fortunate than Henry. The whole world has been the stage of his tremendous drama. He is not so guileless and naïve as Henry; he is immeasurably Henry's superior in intellect and political craft. Nor will he be forgotten as Henry has been forgotten, but be remembered as long as men remember a man.

XIX.

Wilson is the victim of the culminating evil forces of history. The supreme opportunity of mankind came, and the opportunity proved greater than mankind. The supreme spokesman of mankind came, and the Idea which he announced was greater than himself. In a real and large sense, the kingdom of heaven was at hand, and he dissipated its presence. While it is true that the world's evil plight is due to the stupendous deception practised upon the President by the diplomats of Paris, it must furthermore be admitted that this deception could never have been practised upon him had not he himself made the first initial compromise with his principles. The diplomats of Paris could never have betrayed Wilson had not Wilson first been by Wilson betrayed. Doubtless he now knows this himself, and his breakdown is probably the result of the knowledge—of the great inner conflict ensuing it. But it constitutes a tragedy no less vicarious, no less redemptive to the world. It is a conflict before which all men should bow the head, a tragedy before which the gods themselves go softly.

XX.

And now the workers of this tragedy—the peacemakers of Paris—are reaching the limits of mortal infamy by evilly persuading the peoples to visit upon Wilson the punishment for their incomparable treachery, their own depraved diplomacy, their own bestial bondage to the usurers. They would now shield themselves from the wrath of the peoples by turning that wrath upon the head of their victim. They begin to discern that, in overthrowing Wilson, in falsifying his principles and bringing them to derision, they may have overthrown themselves and the civilization they so well represent and reveal.

Yet it is the Conference of Paris, it is not Woodrow Wilson, that will stand judged and condemned before the final assizes of history. It is not Woodrow Wilson, it is the betrayal and destruction of Wilson, that has brought the world to its present pass. It is not the Fourteen Points, it is the repudiation of these Points, that sent the nations walking together in hell.

Yet the ideal which Paris brought low will again be lifted up. The Conference, even by the evil which it has done, has set the eyes of the peoples upon a goal rrom which these eyes will nevermore turn. The ideal of a world-state, of a universal community of man, will grow and glow and ultimately command the will of each people. And the European chancelleries, the American politicians, who set themselves against this divine convergence of the nations are fighting against the stars in their courses.

XXI.

For the root-fact of the present world crisis is this:— that the different groups of mankind can none of them continue to exist separately. We shall soon see that, whether as nations or as social groups, we are so together caught in this crisis that there is no such thing as national or group extrication. The recognition and realization, on the part of all of us, of the universal community of man has become the only ground upon which any of us may survive. That humanity is one indivisible body, one spiritual and economic organism, has now become manifest. Not one of us as individuals, not one of us as nations, can any longer prosper at the expense of other individuals or nations. The fate of everyone of us is—and ought to be—involved in the fate of every other one. We must now together—the whole family of man—through the mobilization of the world's total fund of good-will—through the utilization and mutualization of the world's industrial potentiality—we must now together work out one tremendous salvation, or together go down into one depthless perdition.

Now the vision of all this social unification of the world is what has dimly emerged from Paris—emerged despite the ignorance and incompetence, the hypocrisy and mendacity, which there squandered the largest moral fund which mankind had ever brought together in one time and place. And, after a time, even if it be but after a century of unimaginable death and dread and darkness, the vision shall possess the peoples and prevail unto its factual fulfilment. And this fulfilment—the transformation of his vision into planetary fact—will trace its initial compulsion back to the words of Wilson.

XXII.

Black omissions will stand against Wilson, it is true —things less understandable, things more reprehensible, than his surrenders at Paris. That he should have failed to affirm and maintain the most elementary constitutional liberties of the American people; that he should have looked complacently upon the creation of an American Reign of Terror that would have shamed the last of the Russian Czars; that he should have permitted the right of asylum, freedom of discussion and even of thought, to be driven from the land, to say nothing of the deportation of some whose only sin was that of a literal belief in the obligations laid upon them by the teachings of Christ; that he should have kept by his side such a national deformity, such a supreme exemplar of contempt for law, as the incumbent of the office of the Attorney-General; nor only have kept the *difforme*, but have allowed his verminous creatures to mob and ravage the homes and offices of our citizenry—all this will weigh heavily against Wilson in the assizes of a saner and sweeter national future. It will also stand darkly against him that he did not, upon his return from Paris, proclaim a general amnesty and open the prison-doors of all who had been put in bonds for reasons of war and policy. And for this will Wilson have to answer above all—for this above all—that he left Debs in prison. Nor is it only the unhappiness of the fact—the fact that so Christly a personality as Debs, a man so natively and ardently American, should be held in foul cells: it is for the stupidity of the thing that Wilson must account— a stupidity phenomenal even for our phenomenally *stupid* times.

XXIII.

Yet, after all has been said—after the accounts are all in and the balance struck—it still remains true that America owes to Wilson more than Americans will for a long time realize. Our American public opinion is now divested of reverence, and its emotions and operations proceed under the Lynch Law laid upon it, not only by the powerful organs of the Appetites and Interests, but by Wilson's own Department of Justice. Yet America is still the land of promise—still the land wherein the oppressions of the world may at last find brave solution. In due time, we may have a ransomed and cleansed public opinion, and consideration and social kindness, running their free course in our midst, then heal our own and the world's present madness. And in those days, Woodrow Wilson cometh into his own place—the place of him who summoned America to planetary shepherdship.

XXIV.

So we come round again, some of us, to the faith of Vienna's broken children. Perhaps it is because we, too, despite our betrayed faith and baffled labors, are but exalted broken children of the down-pressing night. Let it be so: our trust, resurgent and resolute, takes up its transmuted refrain: Wilson has come: and though his word has to-day returned unto him void, yet because he has come, yet because he has spoken, after while it will be well with the world.

For the word which Woodrow Wilson has sounded will go forth again, and go forth beyond mortal recall. It is a word which no compromises with himself or his principles can silence: events have brought derision upon his principles: but the principles persist. The joke as to the present whereabouts of the Fourteen Points is universal: but it is a joke by neither wit nor wisdom begotten. For these Points, betrayed and rejected as they are, have nevertheless irreparably shattered the foundations of all imperialisms, political and economic, in all continents and in all time. It was these that defeated Germany, these that destroyed the Empire of the Hapsburgs. It is these that shall base the rebuilding of Russia. And these shall yet break in pieces the Peace of Versailles. The Fourteen Points, far from being lost, have gone into the foundations of the world: and the world will ultimately build itself anew thereupon.

The peoples international have taken Woodrow Wilson more righteously than he seems to have taken himself. Their faith in the things he stood for exceeds the faith he himself manifested. If he compromised, the peoples will not compromise. Though he fulfilled not his promise, the peoples will fulfil it. Appalled and palsied as they now are, they will never turn back from the gates of new world-life before which they to-day bewildered and embattled stand, and unto which they came at his command. The world will be true to the Wilson to whom Wilson himself seems not true.

XXV.

Thus Wilson wrought better, more fundamentally and vastly, than his knowledge or immediate effort. That for which he at last came to stand is but paltry as compared with what he had already, though unknowingly, provided. The Treaty and Covenant to which he consented are but a place for taking breath, a desperate point of departure. He himself has made them so—has made them but provisional and impossible of perpetuity by the greatness of his prior initiative, by the basic faith he exchanged for a poor and perilous victory.

If it be true—and it is true—that for Wilson the world has paid a great price, it is also true that the price is well paid. For the worst that has been done in the shadow of this man's presence is better than the best that either would or could have been done without him. Without Wilson, with the European powers left to themselves, the world would not yet, and who knows for how long, be committed, as it now is committed, to a world-society of free, foreseeing and effectual peoples. No other hands than his were at once willing and empowered to receive the gift of the Great Idea, and press it upon an assemblage of governments.

XXVI.

Nor need we fear that Wilson himself will be able to prevail against the greater thing than himself which Wilson has done in and to the peoples. Nor against what he has done—against the changed world he has provoked into being—is there any power whatsoever that can finally stand. Despite the mobilization of the Appetites and the low diplomacy which so faithfully served them, despite the evil place which the Conference has won for itself in history, despite Paris and despite himself, Woodrow Wilson has channeled the course of the centuries anew. He has driven the world from its old paths for ever, and beyond its old meridians: its path is hereafter among nearer and more luminous stars.

Yes, if unquestionably he failed, if he was tragically defeated, and though the heart of mankind be stricken through with that failure and defeat, Woodrow Wilson has none the less, paradoxical as it seems, both literally and irrevocably overcome the world. And as a world-creator will he increase through the ages. For the world-faith he conjured into appearing, and which in him became for the first time authoritatively vocal, even it now seems forsaken by himself, even if its way undiscernibly lie through long human night —that world-faith will persist, and persist unfailingly, until it fulfil itself in the nations, healed and wedded, walking together toward the descending City of God.

III.
THE MATTER WITH THE PEACE.

Behold, the Lord maketh the earth empty, and maketh it waste, and turneth it upside down, and scattereth abroad the inhabitants thereof. And it shall be, as with the people, so with the priest; as with the servant, so with his master; as with the maid, so with the mistress; as with the buyer, so with the seller; as with the lender, so with the borrower; as with the taker of usury, so with the giver of usury to him. The earth shall be utterly emptied, and utterly spoiled; for the Lord hath spoken this word. The earth mourneth and fadeth away, the lofty people of the earth do languish. The earth also is polluted under the inhabitants thereof; because they have transgressed the laws, changed the ordinance, broken the everlasting covenant. Therefore hath the curse devoured the earth.

Isaiah the Prophet.

The policy of reducing Germany to servitude for a generation, of degrading the lives of millions of human beings, and of depriving a whole nation of happiness should be abhorrent and detestable—abhorrent and detestable, even if it were possible, even if it enriched ourselves, even if it did not sow the decay of the whole civilized life of Europe. Some preach it in the name of Justice. In the great events of man's history, in the unwinding of the complex fates of nations, Justice is not so simple. And if it were, nations are not authorized, by religion or by natural morals, to visit on the children of their enemies the misdoings of parents or of rulers.

If we aim deliberately at the impoverishment of Central Europe, vengeance, I dare predict, will not limp. Nothing can then delay for very long that final civil war between the forces of Reaction and the despairing convulsions of Revolution, before which the horrors of the late German war will fade into nothing, and which will destroy, whoever is victor, the civilization and the progress of our generation. Even though the result disappoint us, must we not base our actions on better expectations, and believe that the prosperity and happiness of one country promotes that of others, that the solidarity of man is not a fiction, and that nations can still afford to treat other nations as fellow-creatures?

John Maynard Keynes.

III

THE MATTER WITH THE PEACE.

I

THE present evil plight of the world, into the possible extinction of our civilization, increasing is the precise result of the betrayal of Wilson, and of the perjurious repudiation of his principles, by the Conference of Paris. Nor of this fact of the matter can the faults of Wilson be made mitigatory. Not all the things wherein Wilson erred, nor any of the things he lacked, can anywise atone for the guilt of the peace-makers, or cancel the scarlet issues of their perjury.

I use the word perjury because it is exact. For the Entente Powers perjured themselves with a moral insensibility, with an instancy also, that has no parallel: there is nothing in history to put beside their moral malfeasance. They had signed a solemn agreement with Germany to make peace on the basis of the Fourteen Points. The acceptance of these, as contractual principles, was the condition upon which the Germans laid down their arms. The Germans believed—and all the world believed—the signatures to be valid. The contract was as binding, as momentous, as any that was ever entered into between nations. It was infinitely more binding indeed: for no previous contract had been weighted with matters even approaching in importance the contents of this. Never had so strict and heavy an obligation to integrity of intention and action has been laid upon the representatives of governments. Here was an instrument upon the honorable observance of which depended the weal or woe universal. Yet in the face of all of this, without hesitation or apology, without even a gesture of fidelity or sign of any sense of honor, the delegates of the governments associated against Germany violated totally and in every particular their inscribed agreement. They contorted treaties that are the exact contradiction of every syllable of the contractual principles they had signed.

What is worse, we now perceive that the Powers had no intention of keeping their contract at all: It had, in the minds of their representatives, nothing to do with the peace that was to be imposed upon Germany. Into the consideration of the covenantors, during all their dreary and derelict discussions, the covenant itself never came. The Fourteen Points, so responsibly agreed upon, so freighted with the faith of mankind, were not once upon the Peace Table.

Yet these associated Powers had professed to be at war for the establishment of international morality! They continued to proclaim this, even while they were engaged in the execution of an infidelity not only flagrant but fatal to mankind. So prodigious was their perfidy, so ignorant and so irrelevant their total performance, that the moral enormity of the Peace, great as it is, seems betimes obliterated by the greater enormity of the processes by which it was contrived. Even the German violation of the neutrality of Belgium, taken merely as a matter of international ethics, diminishes beside the Entente violation of the covenant with Germany.

Moreover, apart from the question of whose the blame is, and conceding all the difficulties of interpretation you demand, and admitting what you will of the problematical element in the application of the contractual principles, it yet remains true that these principles constituted the ground upon which an ample and enduring peace could have been made—a peace at once merciful and just, at once retributive and redemptive, at once exacting and magnanimous. They just as certainly furnished a law and method whereby these three Old-World continents could have been saved, and whereby the early war-faith of the American people could have been fulfilled, as the Sermon on the Mount furnishes the principles whereby a fraternal and free society may be achieved. And, if ever we have a peace that is peace in truth, it will have to be according to these self-same principles—derided as they now are and their protagonist brought very low.

For the Fourteen Points still stand—they still judge the world. The Entente chancelleries and the American politicians are under no greater delusion — and God knows their delusions are great and many enough—than that of thinking they are done with these Points. We are not done with them, nor shall we ever be. We shall ultimately have to build upon them—upon the principles they embody and by the faith they afford—or by them be ground to powder.

II

Now the failure of Paris has not been wholly interpreted by Mr. Keynes, notwithstanding the extraordinary authority of his book. The deserved authority of that book I would be the last to diminish. His exposure of the workings of the Conference, his synthesis of the economic ruin resulting therefrom, is the work of a master. The book has left practically nothing to be said, so far as its chosen field is concerned. Its facts, with the statement and conclusion thereof, are final. The book will be a permanent and perennial source of unhappiest history.

Yet, so far as Wilson is concerned, Mr. Keynes missed his man entirely; and his estimate of Clemenceau is more clever and convincing than comprehensive. His judgment of these two men hangs together, and it is not final. One is captivated, it is true, by the straight-forwardness wherewith Clemenceau acts according to the cynicism so fundamental to his character and usual opinions. His unabashed unbelief and its frank brutality lay hold of the imagination. And there is that in the mental isolation and incommunicability of Wilson which balks not only imagination but sympathy. Yet a nobler-mooded world than ours, and at the same time wiser-minded, will reverse Mr. Keynes' measurements. Wilson will increase and Clemenceau decrease. Wilson is as immeasurably more than Mr. Keynes was able to estimate as Clemenceau is immeasurably less. Mr. Keynes did not discern the actual mental poverty of Clemenceau as well as the dryness of his soul; nor did he in the least perceive the scope of Wilson's mind, or the vasture of his spiritual being.

Nor do Mr. Keynes' mismeasurements change the fact that Wilson presented to the world, both in his person and in his principles, its supreme decretory or creative opportunity, and that the world's subsequent catastrophe resulted from the rejection of that opportunity by the meagre-minded Conference.

III

Before the armistice, two ways of making peace were open to the victors. One was a swift and workable treaty, following the unconditional surrender of the Germans, and candidly based on the power of the victors over the vanquished. Such a treaty would have accorded with European experience, and especially with German practice. If not destructively drastic, and if quickly made, it would, despite its contradiction of the contractual principles, have secured German acquiesence, and have set Europe going again for mayhap a generation.

The second choice, even if an unconditional German surrender had been first required, was that of a peace motived by a well-considered and mutually acceptable justice, resulting in disarmament and a co-operative Europe—a Europe co-operative not only as between its own members, but also in a redemptive program toward the undeveloped and unprivileged peoples of Asia and Africa. Such a program would have realized the general idea of Wilson regarding the war and the peace.

But after the armistice, no two ways of making peace were open to the Conference. The second way had already been agreed upon. We had formally set our signatures to the contract with Germany to make peace upon the Wilson program; and, on the assumption that our plighted word was good, Germany laid down her arms.

IV

We may, as a matter of academic or historic judgment, discuss whether or no the Armistice was a blunder.

I believe that it was. Nor is this only the conviction of a negligible American. I do not know of a single German who stood out against the old regime during the war, and in whom our hope of a German democracy rested, who is not of the same mind. In a very few weeks, these better Germans contend, the imperial armies would have had to capitulate. The military party would hence never have been able to convince the German peoples they had not been defeated. That they are so convinced, is now a matter of common knowledge. It is the belief of the Germans that they were either tricked or betrayed into surrender; and that, bad as their condition was, the victory might yet have been theirs.

It would have cost, it is true, to have permitted Marshal Foch to encircle the Germans and cross the Rhine. But the Armistice and the perjury, with the long blockades purposed to procure Germany's destruction and Russia's restoration to the Romanoffs, took millions of lives more than the capture of the German armies would have taken. Where Foch would have slain thousands, in the procuring of an indisputable victory, the long treachery of the peace-makers has slain whole populations, besides precipitating an era of dread and of death whose scope none can forsee.

But though the Armistice be debatable as a matter of prior judgment, it had no bearing upon the terms of the treaties to be constructed at Paris. So far as our judgment of the Conference is concerned, the question of the wisdom or the unwisdom of the Armistice is without relevancy. The peace-makers had nothing to do but to keep the covenanted word of the governments they represented. They were assembled, if they were honorable, for the sole purpose of fulfilling the contractual principles agreed upon with Germany. Their work was to search out the precise application of these principles to each detail of the peace, to each economic or political or geographical problem before them for solution. The Conference of Paris had no other honest reason for being.

V

Yet what Paris did was to contrive, in express violation of the covenant, a peace that is not only an apotheosis of hatred and revenge: it at the same time exhausts the predatory possibilities of the victors. The Conference treaties, when judged by the agreement that perceeded them, reach the lowest level of diplomatic and governmental baseness: they constitute the most reprehensible failure of historic man; and they are as inexcusable as they are foul. The Peace they profess to have provided, and the abominable processes by which that Peace came into pretended being, have made the years 1919 and 1920 the most infamous in human annals. It is a Peace so atavistic in its psychology, that Julius Caesar, had he been able to look upon so ignominious a result of twenty centuries of human continuity, would have stood aghast at the base futility of man. Indeed, the Conference of Paris assembled thousands of years before Christ had been born.

The shame of what the Conference has done, the mortal insult of the Peace of Paris to humanity, is not yet comprehended by the peoples. But when they do understand, as at last they will, then the perpetrators of this Peace, with their treason toward Wilson and the nations he would have saved, will be cursed as long as mankind curses evil deeds and their doers. If they are ever forgiven, these peace-makers of Paris, it will be upon the ground that they were fatally predestined to write the death-warrant of a divinely doomed civilization.

VI

The spiritual quality of the Conference was perfectly exposed by the manner of the presentation of the treaties to the enemy delegates, as well as by the general treatment to which these delegates were subjected. It was not merely Mr. Clemenceau's unashamed gloating over the fallen Germans that made Versailles the scene of a grim and ghastly caricature of all that the occasion should have been: it was not merely the lamentable absence of Dr. Muehlon or Professor Foertser from the head of the German delegation—either of whom would, by a word, have quickened in the assemblage at least some sense of the high decency then and there required; it was the lack of even the chivalry of savages toward a fallen foe, the absence of every semblance of either intellectual or spiritual dignity, of any apprehension of the macrocosmic meaning of the meeting and the moment, that places the presentation at Versailles among the meanest manifestations of our common humanity.

Equally mean and hateful, equally active against every hope of either a repentant or a co-operative Middle Europe, was the even greater humiliation to which the other enemy delegations were subjected. The Austrians were summoned long weeks before they were wanted. They were kept as petty prisoners, without information or consideration as to when their time would be ended, or any chance of communication with former friends. Impoverished as they were, they were extortionately charged by the French Government for their prison fare. The sainted Professor Lammasch, who for twenty-five years had been the apostle of international justice and disarmament, who twice presided over the Hague Tribunal, and the latchet of whose shoes his jailors were not worthy to unloose, was not allowed even to communicate with friends in Paris concerning his personal needs. He refused to remain, and returned home, his strong faith in Wilson gone, broken-heartedly to die of the humiliation and cruelty to which his people and himself had been so wantonly subjected.

The presentation of the Bulgarian treaty was amidst a scene of such vulgar insensibility and levity as would have reduced a North American Indian to shame. And the Bulgarians too, likewise the Turkish delegates, had been shuttled back and forth between their distant capitals and Paris without regard to their responsibilities or the destinies of their countries—and also extortionately charged for their prison maintenance.

All in all, crusader against Germanism that I have been, I am convinced that, in case the victory had accrued to the Germans, we should scarcely have witnessed a worse disregard of human life and human feeling than was displayed through all the incredible months of the Conference of Paris—fitly culminating in the candid brokers' meetings of San Remo and Spa. And if this condemnation seems sweeping, it is nevertheless proportioned only to what we had a right to expect of the Conference, and to the predestinative opportunity which it so lightly and so vilely cast away.

VII

I have insisted that the fatal issue of Paris is precisely because of its repudiation of all that Wilson came to the Peace Table to procure. But it is well to turn back a little, at this point, and recall his first purpose toward Germany. A mere formal League of Nations was not, as Mr. Keynes seems to imply, the exclusive or even primary object of Wilson's presence in Paris. He based all his hopes upon the League, it is true, but the crux of his world-purpose was the power of his principles, when particularly and honestly applied, to procure the repentance of Germany. This motived all his earlier dealings with the enemy, and even ante-dated his purpose to interweave the League with the Peace—though neither at home in America, nor abroad in Europe, nor finally at the Conference, was there ever a synthetic or even partial understanding of this German policy.

The first purpose of this policy was, to be exact, retributive and preventative. The German nation must be brought to judgment, and be made to pay, so far as mortal payment was possible, for the abominations she had visited upon mankind—abominations so violent, so vast, that neither the speech nor the imagination of man had been able to comprehend or relate them. Then, having been judged, Germany must be stripped of all power to perpetrate these abominations again. She must, for a time, be put under compelling bonds of international restraint and tutelage.

All this was clear enough in the President's last reply

to Germany's demand for an Armistice. In substance, the President said: "Yes, you may have an Armistice, provided our Allies and the chiefs of our armies consent, but only upon certain encompassing conditions. The first of these is, that we must take such comprehensive precautions as will prevent you from violating the Armistice; or from taking advantage of it to renew the war if the Armistice fails of peace. We can put no trust in your word: in dealing with you, we are dealing with a power in which the sense of honor does not exist. We must therefore practically imprison your armies, rendering you powerless to break the Armistice while it lasts."

Where, in the history of diplomatic procedure was ever such immeasurable but deserved humiliation visited upon a great nation? If the President's reply did not stand the Germany of that time before the world in her moral nakedness, I do not know how else such an end could have been accomplished. With courtesy and kindness, yet with a quite devastating precision, he held up the mirror of mankind before Germany, in order that she might really behold and if possible be made to loathe the reflection of her ugliness, both as a Power and as a people.

In fine, the reply of the President to Germany brought that Empire before the judgment-bar of mankind. He put the German nation in a position that should make it, unless it should straightway repent, both the pity and the horror of the ages—and this because of its baseness, its cruelty, its inhumanity in victory; because of its servility and insensibility in defeat. Our President indeed made of Germany a spectacle over which the gods might well and for a long while weep.

But this was only one phase of his purpose, and a preliminary and comparatively incidental phase at that. And it is because the preliminary or retributive phase was seized upon to the exclusion of the greater and final phase, because so few of the world's accredited leaders beheld his object in its entirety, that there were such tragic misreadings of his last reply to Germany's request for negotiations.

VIII

The President's objective had all along been—not mere military victory, but the *moral* conquest of Germany. From his point of view, Germany's military defeat was but the prelude or the means of her moral and political salvation. It was because this moral and political salvation was the goal of his purpose and his diplomacy, the goal he set before our Allies, that he mingled with an unequalled severity and integrity of speech an undertone of invitation and consideration toward the German people. Woven with his absolute rectitude of speech and action, so far as retribution and justice toward Germany are concerned; woven with his requirement of a complete and unconditional surrender on Germany's part; woven with his insistence upon a political revolution that involved the end of the Hohenzollern dynasty and the Prussian military power: there was a subtly sympathetic call to the German people to change its mentality, to take unto itself a new mind and method toward the world. The President not only wished to punish Germany for the wrong she had done to the nations; he not only wished to compel her to repair that wrong, so far as was humanly possible: he wished to make this punishment redemptive. He wished for a spiritual victory so great that the German people itself would understand and at last rejoice in the punishment, in the judgment that had come upon it, and hence of free choice make all possible amends to the world. He wished not only to save the world from Germany: he wished to save Germany from Germanism.

And indeed, unless Germany herself was saved from Germanism, the rest of the world would not be saved therefrom. If we could not get Germany to see and confess her wrong, then even the completest military victory would prove abortive. We should thus have to keep an international guard over Germany: we could not then admit Germany to the Society of Nations; and thus the world would still be wandering amidst primeval moral swamps and monsters, still traversing the low brutish level betokened by the necessity of human forces devoted to slaughter.

IX

Let me state it once again—that the salvation of the world from the German menace depended, in the last analysis, upon the interior salvation of Germany from her ancient self. And this was equally true that the final value of our military victory over Germany, the real proof that we were worthy of it, would lie in its redemptive power. We must not only win a victory over the German people: we must win the German people to that victory. The victory of the Allied armies, however splendid or complete it might be, would be no victory if, at last, it was not so shaped and applied as to win the approval of the German people themselves. It must carry in it that spiritual quality, it must be interpreted by such spiritual purpose, as would enable the German peoples to see the divine reason for it, and to enter co-operatively into the judgments and workings of that reason.

Now the accomplishment of this redemption of Germany, whereon impinged the political redemption of the world, motived the President's attitude toward Germany—motived, primarily, his whole world-policy. If the mere punishment of Germany were the end of the war on the part of the Allies; or if the procuring of the political and economic impotence of Germany were the end; or were it the mere necessity of placing Germany under a temporary international restraint; then our military triumph, then the whole present crisis of mankind, would prove largely futile, would indeed be trivial, as compared with what ought to be its stupendous divine issue. It would indeed be as if God had experienced the agony of bringing to birth a new human age, to find the age born dead when the agony was done.

Thus it had to be, according to Wilson, that, the war ended, redeeming pity and purpose must mingle with judgment and condemnation in our action toward Germany. If we accepted and practised the President's policy, then it was for us to help the German peoples to find and appreciate their true national selfhood that had both betrayed themslves and shattered the world.

Moreover, months before the Armistice, the German peoples were getting the first glimmerings of how long and how wholly they had been deceived; of how hideously they were imaged in the eyes of the world; of how they had been hermetically sealed against the entrance of any and every truth. And Paris was our opportunity to break that evil seal—the seal put upon them not only by their ancient masters, but by their total history. We were summoned to make our victory the open door of Germany into a new mentality—into a new conception of life, of society, of power, of history.

Our power to transmute German efficiency and strength and will into the service of a new humanity—of a humanity bent upon the fulfilment of a free and federate world—this would decide if our victory were faithful or false. If we were not able to accomplish this regeneration of Germany, then we, too, were in need of regeneration; then we, too must needs cast the thing we call Germanism from ourselves.

And good men were then beholding and lamping the light in Germany. Through Bavaria and the Southeastern States especially, and by no means absent from even Prussia, Germany was in the beginnings of a spiritual awakening. Yet this spiritual awakening constituted a tragedy of nations unlike any other which history afforded. Until Germany repented, she could not have domestic peace: until Germany had domestic peace, she could not know that she needed to repent. It was indeed like unto a tragedy of the gods—as if an Aeschylean drama had been enlarged and transmuted for some cosmical audience, with our planet for the stage.

No less, notwithstanding the immensity of the problem, and its paradoxical elements, we were at that time equal to the solution of even this paradox. We were not caught, as were the Greeks and their gods, in the machinery of an unchangeable fate. For the first time in our history, when the Conference assembled at Paris. we mortals were in a position deliberately to decree the future: we were able collectively to lay our will upon our world—to direct, or at least began to direct, the course and the processes of our common evolution.

XI

For use to this end, the Conference had at its disposal two great human values—values which had never before bulked so large. The first of these was the indignation, ready to be formed into efficient will, against the continued exercise of irresponsible might. This indignation, rising against the facts of the world-war everywhere, had sprung first from our detestation of all that Germany had done in the lands she had invaded, and from the revelation of her previous perfidious preparations for the conquest of Europe. It was not only the savagery of her soldiery: not only the waste of countries she occupied, and the commission therein of every known and unknown crime: it was the whole German theory and practice of life and government which had awakened a consuming wrath in the heart of the world. And this wrath was reaching out to include all quarters practising the Prussian philosophy, without regard to their professions of contrary principles.

The horror of Germany's war had deepened and widened into a profound detestation of all war. War's confederate woes were effectually fertilizing a great human purpose to end them. War was being exposed and beheld as the foul and cowardly thing that it is in its essence. And the developing perception and hatred of war's real nature had become a great spiritual asset. It was a fund which, had it been intelligently and proficiently expended by the peace-makers upon whose table it was heaped, could have swept war and its evils from the world.

Let us not say that there is no spiritual or regenerative value in indignation of this kind. In its essence, it is none other than the militancy of love—that forthgoing of love which St. John qualifies as the wrath of the Lamb. Let us remember that the Christ who blessed the little children at his knees was the Christ who scourged the traders from the temple. The most intelligent hatred of what Germany had done came from the ministrants of mercy—from such as Nurse Cavell and members of Mr. Hoover's administration.

In dissipating, as it instantly and prodigally did, this universal indignation, this vast human value, the conference largely dissolved the moral nerve of the nations —so much so that the sense of obligation is breaking down in all political and economic spheres. One may reply that war always ends in reaction and dissolution —in the seizure of power by the exploiter; in the abrogation of freedom of thought and speech; in the destruction of individual and social fidelity; in a world of spies and suspicions and suppressions. But, admitting the truth of the reply, it still remains true that, had the ends of the war been in adequate hands at Paris, these ends could have been so shaped as to have been universally regenerative and creative. And it is because there was neither adequacy nor capacity at Paris, neither intellectual understanding nor spiritual apprehension, neither economic knowledge nor political competence, that we to-day dwell in a world that seems demented and damned.

But the malfeasant peace-makers squandered a greater human value, a rarer and profounder spiritual fund. This greater value consisted of the creative desire for righteousness, international and social, which was then mightily and fundamentally moving the nations. When the Conference assembled, there was a mood in the world, there was a transmuting mind, which made possible the creation of a nobler order of relations between nations and social groups. Not in all the epochs and crises of man had the faith of the peoples risen so high; nor had the desire of the peoples been so certainly divine; nor had the human collectivity been so capable of instantaneous advance and achievement. The whole family of men was lighted and stirred with the most potent expectancy of its common experience. Indeed, a world-order that might even have been a veritable approach to the kingdom of heaven was then at hand—if there had been men at Paris to see and seize it.

But there were none to see, none to answer the creative call. Not only the heaped-up wrath against wrong, not only the creative desire for righteousness then universally astir, but the whole spiritual treasure coming forth from the forge and heat of the war was cruelly and crassly dissipated.

XII

Whence we failed—diabolically, devastatingly, completely: we seemed to have left no evil undone that we could do, nor was one of the promised good things done. In the face of Wilson's marvellous summons to his own people, in the face of the valor and the martyrdom of the people who fought the German madness, the supreme opportunity of our collective humanity was abysmally betrayed by the mercenary forces controlling the Conference. Instead of the peace of redemption, we have squalid contrivances, bestial greed, and an idiotic revenge. Instead of a peace formulated by faith in the practicability of what is good, we have a peace formulated by the faith that only the worst that is in man is politically safe or practicable.

XIII

As to Germany, we have not only wrought, we have deliberately and relentlessly sought, her ruin instead of her regeneration. We decoyed her into the armistice by high promises: we have degraded her by our treachery to those promises. We have proved to the German peoples all their military professors had prophesied concerning our rapacity and hypocrisy in case of our victory.

But worse than all, we have denied Germany any place of repentance—and not even God has the right to do that. We have left Germany morally where she was: aye, we have made her worse than she was: we have changed her hate into hatefulness. The great ones of Paris, not only rejecting but resenting responsibility for the German national soul, have distilled a poison more malignant, more deathfully communicable to the nations that were at war with Germany, than was ever produced by the Junker professors.

XIV

So it comes about that we who brought Germany to judgment now stand in judgment before the German peoples. We who were the accusers are now the justly accused. We who were the monstrously wronged have monstrously become the wrong-doers. We who filled the world with our wrath against the German atrocities, with our grief over the slain thousands of Belgium and France, of Roumania and Serbia and Poland, have destroyed millions by our equally atrocious blockades. We who were the judges are henceforth, if measured by the principles of Wilson or by any decent code of human responsibility, the judged and convicted. We who would grant Germany no place of repentance may soon be searching vainly a place of repentance for ourselves.

XV

We shall surely find no mercy-seat at Paris. For the first condition of an acceptable repentance is the purging ourselves of the Peace there made and of the total tribe to which the makers of the Peace belong. Not by these, nor the like of these, nor the quality of mind they manifested, can the world be saved from early dissolution.

For Paris was at once a moral epitome and an intellectual climax of a civilization that puts its premiums upon a corruptible and unperceiving mediocrity—a civilization that gives its prizes to the intellectual serf, to the crawler and the sycophant. Paris demonstrated that the governors and legislators produced by a mere capitalist society are distinctly a defective and delinquent class—a class from which cometh now no good thing to mankind.

If our civilization be not divinely doomed to destruction, if it be still possible to snatch the nations from the pit, or if the times of terror and torture may be anywise shortened, then it must be through a convocation of the peoples themselves—not through existing governments. There, in the bosom of the awakening peoples, nor elsewhere under heaven at this hour, doth the Immanent Christ proceed; and thence only, whether it be to-morrow or in a thousand years, cometh the peace which all the earth desires—a peace wherein the life of man, free and fraternal and glad, may go faithfully and unwastefully on.

IV.

IF FRANCE HAD FORGIVEN GERMANY.

Ye have heard that it was said, An eye for an eye, a tooth for
a tooth: but I say unto you, Resist not him that is evil: but
whosoever smiteth thee on thy right cheek, turn to him the other
also. And if any man would go to law with thee, and take away
thy coat, let him have the cloak also. And whosoever shall
compel thee to go one mile, go with him twain. Give to him that
asketh thee, and from him that would borrow of thee turn not
thou away.

JESUS OF NAZARETH.

When a man has done thee any wrong, immediately consider
with what opinion about good or evil he has done wrong. For
when thou hast seen this, thou wilt pity him, and wilt neither
wonder nor be angry. For either thou thyself thinkest the same
thing to be good that he does or another thing of the same kind.
It is thy duty then to pardon him. But if thou dost not think
such things to be good or evil, thou wilt more readily be well
disposed to him who is in error.

MARCUS AURELIUS.

As a human being, forgive even thine enemies, and recompense
them only by benefits. This generous self-sacrifice will afford
thee the purest joy. Therefore, remember always that this is
one of the finest victories which reason can gain over the natural
impulses, and that a noble man forgets offences but never benefits.

LUDWIG VAN BEETHOVEN.

Better to perish than to hate and fear, and twice as far better
to perish than to make oneself hated and feared. This must
some day become the supreme maxim of every political community.

FRIEDRICH NIETZSCHE.

IV

IF FRANCE HAD FORGIVEN GERMANY

I

WHEN the German power was broken, France was in the ascendant in the affections of the nations. Her associates in the war all accorded her the first place, and none disputed it. If she had then had a conciousness of peoples other than those of her own national body; if she had evidenced a faith other than that of the Prussian faith in sheer material might; if she had shown a modicum of magnanimity towards either her foes or her friends; she could have asked what she would and it would have been given her. For the world granted the value of France, and had fought to preserve it.

Yet France was unable to perceive any equivalent value in humanity. She, too, was conscious of her value, but conscious of this only. The peoples that cared for this value were fighting for them—except in so far as their safety was contributory to her own: it was herself, and essentially herself only, that France fought for; it was to the defence of herself she had summoned the non-German armies of the earth.

Then, on the moment the Armistice was signed, and incarnate in the person and policy of M. Clemenceau, France anew concentrated her interests, her energies, upon France; and, unhesitatingly and unhaltingly, she toiled and intrigued to concentrate upon herself the interests and energies of her associates. It was her own security, her own enlargement, her own indemnification, her own glory and domination, that concerned France exclusively. To this sole end, the new map of Europe was to be made: the future of the peoples was to be subordinated to France in the making of peace: Europe was made for France, and not France for

Europe. That she over-reached herself, that she blindly served both British imperial diplomacy and the Prussian Junker, does not alter the fact that for the achievement of her ends she sought to put the world under every kind of tribute.

So, when the Son of Man came to Paris in the autumn of 1918, he found no faith in the city, neither in the land whose mind Paris reveals and is. France was destitute of any conception or notion of a security procured through the operation of any other principle than that of the Prussian. She believed in no might except that of her armies, or of an economic stranglehold upon her enemies. She had neither impulse nor policy making for conciliation or redemption, nor any confidence in one. Nor from the day of the Armistice till now, has she given sign of any spiritual faith or quality dwelling in the midst of her national mind or its motivities and methods.

Consequently, France has pursued the salvation that is destruction. The course she has taken, far from insuring her against future assault, inevitably dooms her to war and exhaustion. She has clutched at the phantom of security, and let the substance go. The barbed economic and military entanglements with which she has tried to surround herself are as ropes of sand. The security she has demanded—and obtained, so far as she was able—is an illusion and an imbecility. Her peace of revenge is a peace of every kind of ruin—spiritual, military and economic. The law that might have given her a certain and beneficent security, the law that might have given a new life and history to Europe, of this law France apparently had never heard. She was so ignorant of the true nature of peace that she had not learned the first letter of its alphabet. She staked her future on her power to kill and starve her foes instead of upon a power to reedem them by a generous and gracious justice.

Moreover, it is not only her own disaster France has wrought: laying upon Europe and Asia the law of an essential hatred, founding their future in a mutual and infidel distrust, she has visited these continents with wars without end and with woes immeasurable; and the reaction of her policy has been ruinous to America as well. The moral catastrophe of French diplomacy to the world is at least equal to the moral catastrophe of the German military assault upon humanity. Not more than the Prussian war-makers and professors have the French politicians given one good or saving thing to Europe, one good or saving direction to the new nationalities. Bad as was the German pre-war penetration of Europe, equally bad has been the French military and diplomatic penetration since the war's fabled conclusion.

II

It becomes clear, as the evil days increase, that France never perceived what she was at war with, never visualized her real enemy. It has been her cry, it is still her protest, that she alone knows the German. But the actual German peril—to herself and to the world—is exactly what France did not and does not know. As bad as the German marauder was, France did not even know the worst of him: and she is to-day as ignorant of her foe as she was before he fell upon her farms and villages. She has not conquered, she has not fought, she has not seen, the real German enemy. Indeed, it is the German enemy who has conquered France, laying waste her national soul.

France saw the objective facts and factors of the war: she tabulated and contemplated, again and again, the German's military quantities and qualities: she calculated—calculated overmuch indeed—what reparations she might exact for the wrongs and the ravages the German had inflicted upon her. But these objective facts and factors did not constitute the injury that ultimately mattered. The German injury to France went infinitely deeper than was indicated by her demolished towns and shattered industries; by her tortured citizens, her murdered priests, her ravished women, her slain children; by atrocities so grievous as to make the humanness of our humanity seem questionable.

The thing that really mattered was this—the poisoning of the soul of France by the German national doctrine. That France should have become Prussian-minded —even though recasting the Prussian mind in the terms of the French temperament; that France should have conceived her safety as consistent only with Germany's debasement; that France should have come to base her future prosperity upon the condemnation of seventy million Germans to economic servitude, if not to extinction through starvation; that France, furthermore, should exact from her fallen enemies their uttermost farthing; that thus Germany succeeded, even in her downfall, in creating a political and military France in her own Prussian image; —such was the real German atrocity—an atrocity visited upon the inmost being of France.

The war that Germany made was more than military: she psychologically assaulted the whole moral front of humanity. And against that German assault neither France nor the nations associated with her were adequately armed. She and her allies were called to the battle-fields they did not know, and which their eyes had never been trained to accredit or survey. The German had surveyed these fields materially and exactly, but the warfare he waged thereon was with other than national weapons. We needed other than material weapons for that warfare, and we did not have them. We needed to be armed with an intelligence as finally and robustly spiritual, as tremendously lucid and illuminating, as that of the German was satanically shrewd; nor only shrewd, but lit and cruel with fires infernal.

We do not even yet understand the psychology of the German assault: how Germany, in the pursuit of her purpose to possess the world, was the undoubted user of forces—of which we knew practically nothing —which made for the mental depression, the moral unreason and the dismantled manhood, of persons or peoples against whom they were directed. These are the oldest and evilest of forces, inherited from the imposturous but crafty magicians of her primitive forests, her mediaeval towns; but forces which she had modernly reduced to a dark and masterful science. Germany had developed, in ways subterranean and unthinkable to other peoples, and to an incredible degree, a penetrative power for collective hypnosis, a definite and dominative metaphysic of mass suggestion. And this power was able to motivate every imaginable means, to attach to itself and to operate every sort of human occupation or process—whether the process were mechanical or abstractly intellectual, whether the occupation were menial or required large abilities. Sources of credit, industrial ownerships, instruments of war, seats in universities, works on philosophy, text-books in foreign schools, religious and scientific societies, verbal fogs and trackless confusions, doctors and nurses and governesses, housemaids and butlers and clerks, antiquarian bookshops and modernized pharmacies—these, and innumerable other agencies and agents, were all primary and occult purveyors of the German Idea, of the Prussian's estimate of himself and the world.

Whence we were at war, in our fight with Germany, not with mere material weapons, nor yet with the German Idea only, menacing as that Idea was to humanity's moral existence: we were at war, literally and not figuratively, with powers which Saint Paul long ago declared to proceed from the thrones and principalities of darkness—powers which, in their genesis and activities, constitute the very genius of evil.

To have withstood these evil powers, prophetic reasoning was needed by our governments, and a moral nerve also, beyond any high requirements of the war's military issues or crises. We needed vast and concentrated powers of discernment which neither France nor any of us possessed. Indeed, among all of us who fought the German armies or the German Iedea, it was a new and profound spiritual precipitation which the shock of the German assault should have produced—if the world were not to be lost, after all, and the whole family of men go down into darkness.

But no such spiritual precipitation occurred. We who were in arms against Germany were no more prepared to deal with her military defeat, with the sequent psychological struggle in which our war with her had engaged us, than we were prepared, in August, 1914, to meet the march of the German hordes across the body of Belgium into France. We had been able, despite our lack of preparation, to mobilize our peoples for war —to bring that war to its seemingly successful issue. But there our preparations ended: and there, apparently, ended our capacity to prepare. Our rulers and leaders were incapable of mobilizing the peoples for the mightier task of making peace.

IV

I have pronounced the word peace. In truth, however, the war only began when the war ended—I mean the essential war against the essential German evil. For this greater war, infinitely more fateful than the war that ended before the Rhine, we had neither knowledge nor arms, neither eyes nor ears. The weapons of the powers of darkness could only be met by the weapons of the powers of light. And we not only had not the weapons of light: we were unable to distinguish light from darkness. When the higher bugles sounded, trembling with eternal judgment, we heard them not, but flocked to feast upon the body of the visible enemy; and while feasting upon his body, while establishing frontiers in three continents according to our respective powers to seize the sources of wealth, the evil spirit that drove Germany against humanity entered into humanity and possessed it. British imperialism, French militarism and finance, the American reaction and renunciation of liberty —these are all according to the evil that was Prussian. We who thought ourselves the victors have suffered the saddest and most predestinative defeat that has come to mortals in the course of their recorded history. In all that really matters, and regardless of what now becomes of Germany, the Prussians have won the war.

V

If France had but known the things that made for her peace, she would have sought, first, the redemption of Germany, and, second, the spiritual unification of Europe. She would have forgiven Germany's sins. For this was the first law, the first wisdom, of the statesmanship needed at the moment of Germany's surrender. This forgiveness of Germany's sins was the sole self-defence left to France, and the sole salvation of Europe.

Consider, looking at France alone for the moment, the evil of having a seething and rotting Germany upon her borders—a Germany whose only preservation would lie in returning to her ancient masters and their regime —and set over against this the attitude of a reconciled and repentant Germany. In which, forsooth, did the security of France and the regeneration of Europe lie?

If there had been but one mighty man in France to manifest the statescraft, the spiritual strategy, the political shrewdness, which this forgiveness required for its effectuation,—if there had been one such man to open the eyes of France,—I think France and the world might have followed him. And following him, France would have put the Prussian beyond the pale of return, securing her frontiers for all time; nor archangels with flaming swords could have made them securer. No bristling defences or barbed entanglements, no fleets of the air or far-firing guns, no new and unimaginably devastating modes of death, would have given France such protection as it was in her power to give herself through one redemptive gesture, one magnanimous movement. If she had but looked beyond her apparent self-interest, so morbidly and sordidly conceived, to a Europe needing no strategical frontiers, to a Europe then willed to have done with war, to a Europe of spiritually and economically confederate peoples instead of to a Europe contorted and divided into states vassal to herself, France would have become messianic among the nations, binding the world to her defence by beautiful bonds unbreakable.

VI

It seems indeed fantastic to speak of the politics of forgiveness to the councils that begot the Peace of Paris. Yet the forgiveness of sins is a law written in the constitution of things, and fundamental to social or individual being.

Forgiveness is no priestly prerogative, no mere council of perfection, no pietistic precept or phenomenal virtue, no mythical performance or mystical observation. It is the only principle by which the world or the individual can go on. It accords with the divine indifference that fetches all good things to our feet, that bears all evil things hence.

Nor else can good come and evil go. The sun must either shine equally upon the just and unjust or quit shining. The rain must descend equally upon the good and the evil or its fountains dry up. The man must work for the well-being of his enemy or be destroyed by himself. The nation must redemptively and effectively forgive its foes or be fatally infected with their evils.

The forgiveness of another's sins, of the wrongs done to oneself, is a fundamental condition of self-preservation: not only the preservation of one's spiritual selfhood, but also of one's physical being, of all that makes one's life worth while. To cherish the memory of evil done to oneself, even though the evil be of unimaginable magnitude, even though the whole world has participated in perpetrating it, is eventually to commit spiritual suicide. For he who thus persists in the remembrance of wrongs he has suffered poisons his whole being, deranges his total mentality—indeed so disorders his life and its relations that he can no longer think or act sanely.

The same is true of a nation. A nation cannot make an asset of the most atrocious wrongs against itself without doing itself a greater wrong. To make deeply suffered wrong a national memory, above all to make it the substance and coin of its calculations for the future, is to work within itself a destruction beyond the power of all its enemies to accomplish. A nation can act sanely, can soundly and durably develop, only through the intelligent and systematic effacing of inflicted wrongs from the national memory. There is no health, there is but disease, in revenge or even in retribution irredemptively exacted. The nation that hates is in hell and is devouring itself.

VII

I have spoken of the law of forgiveness as inherent in the constitution of man's universe—as a law everywhere operative and self-enacting, as a law continually and granitically grinding out its judgments. It is not a law whose sovereign operations the man or the nation has any choice about: our choice is limited to obedience and life or disobedience and death. It is not open to us to choose whether or not we shall have to do with the law: the law has to do with us whether we choose to do with it or not.

Unless there is a way of getting out of the universe, there is no way of getting from under the jurisdiction of the law of forgiveness. The law works ceaselessly on, either working out our individual redemption and the world's redemption, in co-operation with us, or collisionally working out our ruin and our contribution to a possible ruin universal. One of the chief causes of the dissolutions of civilizations has been the vindictive character of their customs, their laws, their conceptions of justice—or, to put it in terms of my theme, their collision with the law of forgiveness.

VIII

To forgive one's enemies is to fight them intelligently and to triumph over them. To fail or to refuse to forgive one's enemies is to yield to them the victory. The only victory that eventually overcometh evil is the perceptive forgiveness of the evil-doer. If one could forgive enough, if a nation could forgive enough, he or it would bear away the sin forever from the forgiven man or nation.

So the greatest wrong our enemies can inflict upon us, the only wrong in fact, is in our permitting them to create hatred and bitterness and revenge in our own hearts, in allowing these to motivate our action. If we can prevent our enemies from preventing us from loving them, from wishing them well and seeking their redemption from the evil they have done, we have withstood them and conquered them eternally. But if once they compel us to hate them, if once our reaction runs to revenge or irredemptive retribution, if once we are moved to stop with the imposition of a merely legal or Roman justice, then it is our enemies who have won and ourselves who have lost. No matters it how inclusively we may have destroyed their armies; nor how low we have brought their institutions; nor with what waste we have visited their lands; nor how exhaustive the tribute we have exacted from them; it is no less they who have won and we who have lost. It was Carthage that destroyed Rome, in the end. It was the soul of Carthage, entering into the soul of Rome, that finally destroyed the Empire.

IX

It will commonly be said that France could not forgive Germany until Germany first repented. But forgiveness is not conditioned upon repentance. More often, repentance results from forgiveness. We are to forgive in order to produce repentance. We are to forgive, also, in order to consume within ourselves the wrong done against us; so that in our conciousness the wrong no longer exists, no longer predicates our attitudes or actions toward the wrong-doer. In so far as we are able to do this, we bear the wrong away from those who have committed it. Thus by this law—absolute to an actual follower of Christ—the German atrocities laid upon France an opportunity, and an inescapable responsibility, for Germany's redemption.

Moreover, at the time of their defeat the German peoples were, as I have already said, mooded for repentance. They at that time desired to have done with their past—desired to be convinced that they had been duped and betrayed and destroyed by their rulers. It may have been but for a moment that Germany was so mooded; but it was one of those great moments which, when instantly seized, change the course of human evolution. If France had seized the moment—if she had then acted forgivingly towards Germany; if she then sought to save these peoples at the heart of Europe from their darkening teachers and darker history; I am certain they would have responded with an instancy and urgency that would not only have changed their mind toward an astonished world, but would have surcharged the world with a new mind and mood. France would have armed Germany spiritually while disarming her militarily. The power of the Junker would have dissolved in a night. The teeth of the German terror would have been drawn for ever. And France, leaving Germany without excuse, would have made herself the conscience—yea, the very Christian conscience—of mankind.

X

Yet France, as if seized by some stupendous fatality, has pursued the precise things that make for her perpetual peril, if not her ultimate perdition. She has banished peace from her frontiers, peace from her path, peace from the world. Instead of curing the German disease, she has preserved it and nourished it. Instead of lifting the curse from Germany, she has taken it upon herself. Instead of lifting the German curse from Europe, she has laid it upon the whole family of nations. And she has given the fundamental excuse which the Prussians needed in order to justify their past, and to carry that past into the future. She is systematically creating the German revenge and recreating German militarism.

And it is impossible to believe that France is so blind, so unintelligent, as not to know this. It is impossible not to believe that France, or the military-financial party that now possess France, is not deliberatetly and of a set purpose pursuing a course that make for perpetuating the German military menace. For the German menace is the justification of the French militarism for its own perpetuation. It is furthermore a course that, in provoking German resistence, brings about a French excuse for Germany's complete subjugation, and prepares the way for converting the Continent into a French military dominion.

Thus the problem of militarism has been transferred from Germany to France. The French military missions are now commanding practically all the armies of Eastern Europe, except those of Trotsky. It is no secret that even Von der Goltz on the Baltic, at the very time when the Supreme Council was demanding of Germany his recall, was acting in accord with France and the British War Office.

XI

So the last result of the French peace is this—that if Germany survives, it may be by a restoration of the Prussian regime. There are even those in France, and in Great Britain as well, who are secretly wishing and working for such restoration, under the imagination that they are thereby destroying bolshevism. But this, too, is a phase of the blindness engulfing the Entente politicians and soldiers. For the old regime once restored in Berlin, will become the support of a compromised Russia; and Germany, becoming thus Russia's protector, will also become the exploiter of the vast Russian resources, and will thence effect the reorganization of Europe according to the German mind. It is possible that this result, so momentous, so unforseen, so stupendously evil in its possibilities as to be beyond mortal calculation, has already been potentially established, and is now beyond the power of the Entente to disestablish or recall. And this will be the work of France—of the France that did not know the things that made for her peace—the France that did not know the politics and the justice of forgiveness.

XII

The Table of Principles which Wilson brought to Paris, and which was there abandoned—abandoned by himself if you will have it so—was essentially constructed according to the law of forgiveness, and predicated the quality of justice that issues therefrom. If the rulers of France had been possessed of true political perception, they would have recognized the certain and even providential security these principles provided — not for France only, but for Europe and the world. But the purpose for which Wilson came to Paris was not realized. It had not the faith, the sincere or actual support, of either Europe or America—to say nothing of the special opposition, both open and secret, of France.

Yet, paradoxically enough, and mayhap even yet redemptively to our civilization, the very consequence of France's failure, of the Entente infidelity to the fourteen Principles contractually signed, is a plight of the world so evil, so malignly increasing, that there is no extrication from it for any people except through a policy of mutual forgiveness on the part of all peoples. *International forgiveness is now the sole ground of hope for the world.* The nations must forgive one another's debts, or together go down into financial and industrial perdition, into economic servitude or general starvation. They must now forgive one another's atrocities and revenges, moral and material, including the low diplomacies, the lewd intrigues, the black treasons they have all habitually practised upon each other, or else become a guerrilla-world and a jungle. In this forgiveness,—in the justice that is identical therewith,—is the sole force able to lift the curse whereunder the world-order staggers to dreadful doom. And alone in this justice,—in the forgiveness that procures it,—in the love whence it comes,—waits the land of the world-heart's desire.

V.
GERMANY MUST REPENT.

The "Vernichtungswille," the will to destroy all those nations which are in the way of Germany's unlimited political, economical and moral expansion, all those nations which do not accept servitude, economical as well as moral, lies at the bottom of the whole problem. This is the inmost spring of the German's actions towards foreigners, even if it is often unconscious. No other nation ever put this criminal passion into a moral and even a mystical theory like the Germans did. Therein lies the political obsession of the German, and when we want to get at the bottom of the whole problem, we cannot limit our judgment to what archives gives us.

PASTEUR LOUIS FERRIERE.

Germany attempted to find a pretext for her invasion of Belgium in the hypothetical intention of France to march through Belgium along the Rhine, and in pretended occurrences which were supposed to prove the reality of this intention. Not one single sound proof can be adduced of France's violation of the German frontier; it has even been established on the German side that the French plans of mobilization did not foresee the invasion of Belgium. As far as the Belgian mobilization is concerned, the plan of an equal distribution of the Belgian forces on all frontiers was only altered to a massing of troops in the East after the German invasion was known to be a fact.

And Germany's moral obligation is the confession of the wrong done to Belgium, and the necessity of reparation, so far as that is possible. For many extreme militarists, and Pan-Germans this confession may be a bitter pill; they will point with scorn to Great Britain and France, in which countries there is no inclination to discuss or confess their own misdeeds. In the history of the world, however, every nation is responsible for itself. Insistence upon the unrighteousness of Great Britain and France does not absolve another nation from its moral duty. Each nation must begin the cleansing process with itself; and one or another must make a beginning. If each is going to point to the obduracy of another, we shall never acquire the spirit which ought to inspire the common life of the League of Nations. There is absolutely no doubt that Great Britain and France have heavy sins upon their consciences. It should be our privilege to set a good example to the nations by an honest resolve to repair the wrong which we have done.

M. ERZBERGER.

V

GERMANY MUST REPENT

I

THE Entente Powers have made it difficult—in fact shameful—to speak of the sins of Germany. And the difficulty is enhanced by every new action or decision of the Entente representatives. The Supreme Council—the mere brokers' agency which it has become—which indeed it ever was—is perpetrating bargains so brazen, treasons so incredible, that the peoples stand astonished and dumb, the capacity for indignation exhausted. Behold San Remo:—the Supreme Council,—gambling in last chances,—gaily stakes the destinies of three continents on the capture of new supplies of oil. Witness the throwing of the Polish people upon the table of the gamesters:—the starving Poles, typhus-stricken also, and at the risk of national extinction, march to the blackmailer's music— stabbing Soviet Russia in the back while the British Prime Minister negotiates with that same Russia for a Trader's Truce. How can an Anglo-Saxon speak of Germany's sins, of Germany's need of repentance?

Add to this our refusal of a place of repentance to Germany. Ever since we signed the contractual Fourteen Points, we have pursued a course that could not be else than hardening to the German heart. The circumscribing perfidy of all that the Conference and the Supreme Council have done, can have no other effect than that of robbing Germany of every place of repentance.

Nor can we forget that there was a time when we who were at war against her could have fulfilled that mood. I have twice brought that time forward in this book, and I do not wish to leave it in the background. I do not wish to mitigate the folly of our failure to avail ourselves of that fortnight wherein we might have initiated a new Germany. We not only did nothing to invite, we did everything to destroy, every impulse for repentance on the part of the German peoples during those formative and fateful days following the Armistice. Neither am I ignorant—nor would I leave anyone ignorant—of earlier times when we might have saved Germany and did not. When, for instance, Kurt Eisner and his remarkable colleagues established the Republic of Bavaria, and when they appealed to our President to procure for them some small or even tacit support, we could have made this very able revolution, with the superior men who wrought it and who were then governing Bavaria, our *pou sto* for a moral invasion and conquest of Germany. We were apostate to our opportunities: the Prussians assassinated Kurt Eisner: another minister, a very lovable and efficient man, went insane with dissappointment; other good men of Munich committed suicide and still others were slain. Through a pseudo-bolshevist uprising, Bavaria passed completely into the possession of the Prussians. And this sad infidelity to divine opportuinty leaves upon us a guilt from which we, too, can be cleansed only by repentance.

Yet when all the admissions have been made, when we stand fully clothed in the shame that is ours, it still remains true that Germany must repent, if we are to find or to keep the lost balance of the world. Germany's responsibility for the initiation and continuation of the war will have to be recounted, in order that we may have some synthesis of the causes of the present fall of mankind. All the evil we have so deeply spread abroad through the world, cannot release Germany from her responsibility for letting loose the war and for the hardness wherewith she pursued it to the end. Even granting that Poincare and Russia first spread a trap for her feet, it was Germany herself that sprang the trap.

It was Germany that began the war, and for the guilt there is no palliation. There lived just one man who could have prevented the catastrophe and did not—that was the German Emperor. There was just one people that could have withheld the world from the red abyss —the German people. Nothing can excuse this man;

nothing excuse this people. They can and must be forgiven; but nothing but repentance, nothing but a changed mentality, can bear away their sin. No matter how many and great the previous or subsequent sins of the Entente Powers, no matter how hateful and avaricious our treatment of Germany and her allies, it was none the less her hands that loosed the foul forces; and nothing can cleanse those hands except her full confession, and a consecration of herself to the tasks of repentance. Nor repentance for only the material wrongs —for these are comparatively trifling—but for the profounder and far-reaching spiritual damage done to mankind.

No, it was not merely war that Germany loosed upon the world: she provoked the wickedness now wasting the souls of nations. Hence upon Germany rests the responsibility for becoming, as she can become, a healer of the nations she has brought spiritually as well as materially low. Let her therefore not listen to friends who would withhold her from repentence and confession. When English and American pacifists speak thus to Germany, when Mr. Morel and Mr. Trevelyan warn her against repentance, bidding her balance her sins against the equal sins of France and Anglo-Saxondom, these good men are rendering her the worst service, are doing her the last injury. They are sealing the perversion of the German national soul.

III

It will be said, over against this, that there were times when we could have nogotiated with Germany a peace which would have averted the ruin. But even had we made peace on one or the other of these occasions, no change of the German mind was in question. The peace would have been one of negotiation, one of temporary or mayhap permanent abandonment of the German world-purpose, but involving no repentance or confession. Germany looked to the proposed Peace Conference through eyes that beheld things antipodal to those beheld by the Entente and by America. A conference in which Germany would then have participated would not have procured peace. She intended to sow the seeds of distrust between delegate and delegate, between nation and nation—even between her own allies. Having made the conference a place of discord, having infected it with all the elements that are the opposite of peace, then out of the diplomatic dispute and disorder she would have gained the last possible advantage. If she could have only gotten us to a premature table of peace, she would there have created a state of prolonged complexity, such as would have worn out the moral patience of the world; and meanwhile she would have gained, through her power for collective hypnosis, much of what she had lost in the field. The peace conference that Germany besought during the war would have been nothing else than a phase of her struggle for dominion.

But Germany did not get the conference she then sought, and to no peace table did she afterwards arrive. When, later in the war, and before her final downfall, she would have made a more penitential peace, the Entente politicians, already consecrated to the Appetites, had planned the military subjugation and exploitative division of Asia and Africa, as well as of Europe beyond the Rhine; and, when the Conference of Paris met, no place of repentance was provided for Germany.

IV

Germany did not essentially change her mind during the war. And the mind of the German, in all its motions and methods, even in the stuff of which it is made, seems radically different from the mind of other Aryans. Exact only when it expresses itself mechanically or automatically, and in this respect even super-exact, it loses itself utterly in any attempt at moral perspicuity or vital prospection: it has no measurements for the essential values. The German mind hates precision in the things that matter: it prefers and revels in the fog. One definition must be such as to require two, and two to require four, and four to require eight, and eight to require sixteen. In this eternal indulgence in definition that never defines the German mind is at home; and therein responsibility disappears.

Scrutinized historically and presented baldly, the German cannot be recognized as other than a pathological type. His mentality is not moral in the sense that the English or the American mentality *may* be moral. If we Anglo-Saxons are normal, then something—it does not appear where or how or what—has caused a psychological flaw in the evolution of this people; or else there was a slip in the making of the German—something left out in his creation. Whichever it is, whether accidental or genesial, something is inherently amiss in his mental constitution. The German, in his present stage of development, cannot think directly and therefore morally. He motivates himself in a mental universe into which moral directness or reason has not entered. He still moves, he still has his psychic being, collectively speaking, in what seems like pre-human nature.

Thus the German, if you track him down, if you get beneath his deeds or behind his words, commonly reasons that whatever accomplishes his ends as an agent or citizen of the State—which ends he always assumes to be super-right—is both mystically and scientifically justifiable. No matter how reprehensible the means, there is no responsibility higher than these ends that can claim his confidence. I do not mean that this is the creed which each German has thought out and confessed; but I do mean that this is the mental stuff of his conscious or unconscious motivity and volition. The sheer might that achieves the thing in view, the force efficient and sufficient for its own fulfilment in the conquest of other forces, is his supreme yet irresponsible good.

Nor is the German creed only according to the philosopher. For just as Hegel reports the stark might of the Prussian State as the Divine Presence, so the German peasant, the German priest, the German soldier, the German socialist, before the war, unconsciously regarded every violence or vileness which this monstrously conceived State commanded as the carrying on of a Divine Incarnation. And that the German is affectionate in his immediate family, is in friendly fellowship with his community, is sentimental and romantic and lovable, subtracts not the least from the abnormality and unmorality of the universe his mind inhabits, and whence proceeds the riddle of his actions.

V

Germany's war-time peace missions to Switzerland were so numerous, the procession of them so continuous, that they constituted a veritable clinic for the observation of the German mind; especially did they present an exceptional opportunity for the study of the national psychology in relation to the war and the peace Germany then purposed.

The first and least difficulty the questioner of these messengers observed, aside from their obvious and naive lack of knowledge of opinions outside Germany, was the absence of all sense of responsibility for the war's commencement, continuation and conclusion. Each discussion, without regard to the messenger's intellectual repute, or his high or low official degree, began with the assumption that Germany was misunderstood and wronged, even to the extent of a piteous martyrdom. To this assumption the messenger faithfully held, even when it was accompanied by admissions, always meagre and equivocal, that Germany herself had been betimes remiss. And wherein she was remiss, mind you, it was because of deceptions practised by jealous neighbors upon this all too trustful, too childlike a people. The messenger placed the responsibility for the war's beginning and ongoing and ending upon England or America; never upon Germany was either responsibility placed.

Moreover, Germany must be preserved from *discovering* that the responsibility was hers. As an instance, an eminent and official German of high intellectual quality—a German whom I had long held in affectionate admiration—continually sought to show me that the war must be so ended as to save Germany from the humiliation of confession. The preservation of Germany's national pride, more than the revelation of righteousness to her people, was basic in all this good man's quest for a better German future. Well aware as he was of the historical abnormality of his race, admitting it candidly enough in our discussions, yet so thoroughly German was he that he could conceive of no peace except one that would save Germany from self-accusation. Nor labored he the less for this peace—a peace that could only have been a curse to his people had he achieved it —when I convinced him, as I was sometimes able to do, that upon the ground of their self-accusation and confession rested the only hope and help of the German peoples.

VI

There was more than evasion on the part of these Germans: there was an element of downright derangement. Despite your will to doubt the evidence of your close experience and long observation, despite your sincere and determined search for some other and more desirable explanation, you are forced to the conclusion I have already stated—that the German brain did not function morally in national or political matters: it did not seem made for distinctions between right and wrong as we understand those distinctions. In the mentality of this race, whenever and wherever the state was involved, there was no line between the base and the treacherous and the brutish on the one side, and the faithful and honorable and truthful on the other. You confronted only a ponderous and impenetrable fog between the two; or else a primitive and serpentine cunning. You found, in even eminent German professors—and the more eminent they are the more surely you seem to find it—an intellectual drivel and trickery so incredible as to create the feeling that you were wandering in a realm of solemn and inexplicable idiocy.

VII

A quality of the German's mind was manifested in his method of political approach and retreat. He began, usually, with a political arrogancy that, until you became accustomed to it, struck you dumb. But when you took this mode of approach for granted and prepared for it, when you drew across the missioner's soul a spiritual lash, then instantly his attitude changed to one of self-debasing entreaty. You became aware, after a time, that he knew nothing else than either arrogance or servility. The moral world that lies between the two, between domination and submission, was hid from his mental eyes, and he had no consciousness of its existence. Whether it were in the realm of government, of military or industrial organization, of university method or public school instruction, the German knew only unquestioned command or unquestioning obedience. The standards that create or stimulate manliness, that require moral candor or directness, that provoke spiritual integrity and stature—these standards were as foreign to the German as the plays of Aeschylus to the Eskimo.

Nor was this curious blend of arrogancy and servility charactistic only of the official or academic individual: it was the attitude of the German collectivity, of the Prussian State toward the world. Germany might perpetrate unimaginable insults and savageries upon other peoples, and be jubilant about them; but the moment she received retaliation in kind, at once the voice of the nation became a whine. And this whine was the constitutive tonality of the German appeals during the war.

VIII

Nor was this mentality a modern phase of the German's evolution. He has had no other racial mind or morality—so far as history and his philosophy show. We have only to refer back to descriptions of the German by marvelling Romans; to what said Julius Cæsar—who so chivalrously admired his other enemies; or to later characterizations of the German by Dante and other great Tuscans. We have but to put the mystical immorality of Fichte's political philosophy beside John Milton's conception of man and the State; or to regard the appropriative quality of the universality of Goethe in the light of the interpretative universality of Shakespeare. Reflect as much as you like, search where you will, you will not find moral masculinity or intellectual manhood, you will not find soundness or erectness of soul, in the general thought or history of the Germans. It is either the whine or the whip you will find—and find as present in German literature and philosophy as in German war and statescraft.

IX

The Germans spoke much, during the war, of their national honor. They would declare themselves ready for any concessions, for the sake of peace, short of what they conceived to be the honor of the German State and name. Yet what they mistook for national honor was a primitive tribal pride. It was the appearance and prestige of power, the outward show of material military might, they were determined to preserve. I did not hear, in the conversations I had with them, the first hint of an honor that was moral—an honor based upon international and national honesty. I did not discern the least sign of a search for national righteousness. I was not able to discover, from the German's quest for what he called a "peace of understanding," the faintest comprehension of fidelity to a promise or a principle. Indeed, honor in the Anglo-Saxon sense of that word, exists not in German political philosophy or practice or national consciousness. We may readily admit—we cannot in truth avoid admitting —the prodigious hypocrisy—the veritable super-hypocrisy indeed—of the Anglo-Saxon as regard his high conceptions: but the German had not even the conceptions.

It was with a great and grievous reluctance I reached this conclusion. I began my war-time discussion with German friends—more lovable to me than any friends I possessed outside of Italy—with the one consecrated purpose of finding some ray of light in Germany, some promise of Germany's salvation within the German peoples themselves. I searched for this light, I groped for this promise, as for hid treasure. But in vain: the light and the promise were not there. There was only darkness, a darkness the German did not dispel.

The salvation of Germany had to come either from repentance or catastrophe: and Germany did not repent, did not change her mind. So the German salvation could come only from the association of nations at war with her—but come, even then, when we had accomplished the yet unapprehended task of casting the Prussian mind from ourselves. Until now, we have not only borrowed the Prussian mind: we have infinitely justified and expanded it.

X

But what were the things whereof Germany needed to repent—still needs to repent—in order to fulfil her true function in the family of nations?

I.—It was Germany's material-mindedness that imaged the super-humanity she pursued—which she even thought herself to have achieved. I am aware, as I say this, that the word materialism has been mouthed out of meaning, and that none are more materialistic than those whose cant about materialism is tiresomely familiar. Yet it is nevertheless true that modern Germany had become the apotheosis of the materialist mind; and of this material mind was the German efficiency—an efficiency, be it admitted, incontestably superior to that of other peoples. The Germans had indeed mastered, had in fact created, a metaphysic of materialism, an occultism of earth-forces, which was the negation of the spirit inwardly striving for the divine becoming of our humanity

Whence it had come about that Germany's teachers and leaders had literally succeeded in creating a god after their own image. They had created a national state of mind, moved entirely by material cause and effect, that had become an essential entity, answering to all the purposes of a fearful and powerful god. And this huge German image, this Hindenburgian god, was begotten by the German mind—by German philosophy, theology and history. Luther and Hindenburg are identical German types, each worshipping a heavenly brute-god who was particularly a fortress for the German peoples in their war with the world. The trackless fogs of Hegel enshrined the same god, the same principle and authority of might; and the same god sat protectingly above the Prussian State. Nor was he less the god of Marx than Bismarck. The principle of authority which Bismarck held was in essence identical with the principle of authority behind Marx. The state which Bismarck conceived was dynastic, and that of Marx collective; but each was based upon the exercise of sheer might; each was a sheer autocracy.

It will be said, and rightly, that material-mindedness is not confined to German frontiers; that America and Great Britain, for instance, are materialistic, and France and Italy also; and that it is rather the materialism of the whole Western World, especially since the time of the Reformation, that has produced the catastrophe. All true. We have all wrought the wickedness that inheres in the materialist mind, and our wickedness is daily waxing worse. But we at least had proclaimed and professed other principles. False as we were to them, and falser still as we are to them to-day, the ideas of a progress wholly spiritual, wholly liberating to the soul of man, were extant among us and had a remnant of active believers. But it was only Germany that had exalted the wickedness of the material mind into a divine righteousness. It was Germany that had peculiarly infected the world with the worship of material forces, and that had laid the law of the material mind upon humanity.

II.—It was a conscript world that Germany pursued; and it was not the military conscription that chiefly mattered; nor even the industrial conscription toward which Germany was moving: it was the conscription of the soul, of the whole man. And this conscription of the whole being of man became the basis of every humanist movement that passed under German direction, every such movement becoming thereby a destructive instead of a creative force.

Such was the case with socialism. I cannot here go

into a history of the socialist movement. I can point only to the long damage done to it by the German mentality —a damage at once political and spiritual, and preventing that leadership of labor to which socialist parties aspire, but which they have never possessed. Springing originally from France, begotten by such minds as Saint-Simon and Fourrier, consecrate and empowered with that idealism so native to French revolutionaries and reformers, the socialist movement was at first vital with early Christian inspirations. But it became a victim of German intellectual conquest. By that combination of spiritual insensibility and intellectual brutality so peculiar to the Prussian mind, Karl Marx and his drill-sergeants drove spiritual impulse, also democracy, from socialist doctrine and propaganda.

Every attitude of Marx toward spiritual being, toward an essential human nobility, was hateful—as instanced by his ugly assaults upon Mazzini, or by the flippancy and puerility of his reference to Jesus. Indeed, Marx was scarcely human: he was a sort of miraculous yet monstrous mental mechanism, combining almost super-human powers of historic and economic analysis with extraordinary intellectual intolerance and personal pettiness. It was the sandbag and bludgeon, the butcher's axe or the prize-fighter's smash, that Marx used upon those who had the temerity to question his conclusions or his authority.

And, to say nothing of spiritual impulse, neither Marx nor his associates ever glimpsed democracy in their perspectives, or pioneered it by their conduct. They had not a single democratic instinct not an iota of actual democratic faith. There was no place in their mental processes, no place in their emotions, where the democratic faith could find lodgement. Marx was himself as much of a despot, was as suppressive of free thought and discussion and being, as any inquisitor ever upraised by church or state.

So he and his kind conquered socialism, thoroughly dehumanizing it in doctrine, thoroughly materializing its impulses and perspectives, thoroughly Prussianizing its organization and procedure. The socialist movement became a body without a soul—aye, even without a body that could be called organic—it was nothing so living as that.

Yet a hierarchy, also, its priests the Luthers and Calvins of materialism. And this materialistic hierarchy imposed itself upon the nations as democratic and international. It was neither. It has never been socialist in essence or fact, never democratic or international, but anti-social, autocratic and anti-national. In its own special sphere, the German Empire, wherein it grotesquely passed as a movement making for social democracy, it adopted all the worst features of Roman Catholic ecclesiasticism, with none of the democratic and spiritual genius at the core of Catholicism. Its conception of socialism was never other than that of a collective Prussian State.

And with what results to mankind! In Germany itself, where, if the socialist party had held fast for four days in August, 1914, it would have made the war impossible, that party passed instantly into the service of the Kaiser in his assault upon humanity. And during the war, the socialist movement throughout the world was an agent, more or less conscious, for the propagation of Prussianism. Indeed, the German people and the real hope of a German socialism had no worse enemy, not even in the Junker, than the fabled social democracy. Capitalism had no politicians more capitalistically-minded than those provided by materialist socialism. The movement which ought to have prepared for the real coming of a new humanness into the life of humanity—this movement became a veritable anti-human apostolate. And the redemption of socialism from the Prussian, and the birth of another spirit than that begotten by Marx and the Prussians, this is the beginning of any socialist wisdom that will hence work the weal of the world's worker, or initiate the commonwealth of mankind. And, to-day, the hope of mankind—if mankind be not already destined for the jungle—is in a regenerate and humanized socialist movement.

And this, let it be said in passing, is what we may expect of Russia. I do not believe the proletarian dictatorship affords any more certain solution of the problem of life and labor than Czarism. I am unalterably opposed to every kind of dictatorship, to every sort of conscript society. Yet I have no fear that the ultimation of the Russian revolution is in either dictatorship or conscription. Whatever and however terrible the phases through which it has passed or may yet pass, whether it for a time dissolve in chaos or pass awhile under the power of the Prussian, or if perforce it politically coalesce with capitalist reaction, the Russian revolution will not remain bolshevist: it will at last end in the bosom of Christ, and in a social order therefrom proceeding.

III.—But Germany's greatest sin—and the sin most unforgivable in the end—is this: her will and her work to disrupt the community of nations—or rather, her will and her work to prevent the community of nations from coming into being, from becoming first a faith and then a fact.

The world is essentially one community of man. It is the relation of household to household in the harmonious village that best prefigures the true inter-relation of nations. It is the affectionate family, in which each gives to each without thought or measure, that is the true microcosm of a whole and happy society.

The realization of such a world-community has been the primal impulses of all epochal movements and changes, such as the eager propagation of the early Christian idea; the English foundations which King Alfred laid; the charter of America's beginnings as a nation; or the French Revolution—still far from being fulfilled, and to-day channelling anew its messianic course.

And though the community of nations has long been a familiar figure of political speech, it has had no place in diplomatic purpose or procedure, no basis in the past historical fulfilments. The realization of the family of man in the common consciousness and conduct of nations is a goal we scarcely yet behold, or at best but follow from afar. It is the goal which Joseph Mazzini hailed —but to an unheeding and unworthy Europe. And it is the goal which Woodrow Wilson beaconed anew for the world.

But entrenched between this goal and the nations, determined on preventing all perception of it, was the German Empire—the Idea upon which that Empire had been built and by which it had penetrated and peverted the world. The preservation and progress of the German's power depended upon his keeping the peoples ignorant of their community of interest; on thwarting the communion of national spirit with national spirit; on the baffling of that feeling after fellowship between peoples and classes which is the most fundamental and finally efficient force beneath the upheaved world to-day.

In striving thus against the spirit that was working for the brothering of the world, Germany committed—literally and not figuratively—the sin against the Holy Ghost. To divide people from people, to divide man from man, and so to divide man from God, in order to build power and dominion upon these divisions—this is the supreme profanation in which both Britain and France are to-day surpassing the German. The mind of man cannot conceive of a sin more generally woeful than this. Beyond this sin against God and man, beyond this sin against the Uniting Spirit eternally striving for the true birth and beatification of man—beyond this Satan himself cannot go: for this is the very genesis and genius of evil. We are here at the boundaries of sin's possibilities; we here reach the frontiers of mortal infidelity.

Thus Germany had become both the Great Denial and the Great Denier. All the ascending movements of history, all its creative changes and currents, all we know of cosmic tendency, all the accredited voices of God and man, have worked and spoken for the realization of the unity of the race, for the achievement of the mutual-membered mankind. And all the effort of Germany, ancient and modern, all the history and practice of Germany, and the very evil faith by which and upon which the Empire was built, were against this striving of the Spirit for self-realization in one human family

—this striving of man for conscious and continuous unity with his one true self.

It will be truly said that other nations have also committed this sin, again and again. Yet other nations have committed the sin shamefacedly, apologetically, knowing it to be evil. Even the hypocrisy of other nations is a tribute to the uniting idea and a discrediting of the dividing idea. But Germany had reduced the sin to a science, and made of it a religion. She had deliberately chosen this uttermost offence against God and man to be her good—to be her golden creed, her national policy, her supreme power, her imperial law, her mighty mystery. She had thus reared herself upon a foundation that is the antithesis of human trust, and by a principle that is the negation of spiritual existence.

XI

Forty years prior to 1914, and unremittingly during the war, Germany applied the scientific method of a penetrative propaganda for the imposition of her will upon the world. She had invested her science of propaganda with qualities and with a craft that partook of mediæcal or Asiatic sorcery. The devious ways, for instance, by which she obtained, the world over, even unto remote and unconsidered regions, control of the sources of credit, in order to direct the mentality of the people dependent upon that credit; the ways by which she possesses herself of educational initiative and procedure in the non-German nations:—all this constituted a strange and insidious metaphysic or occultism of control. This metaphysic of things, this occult use of material forces and educational processes, was something that, up to that time, neither the Anglo-Saxon nor Latin worlds had contemplated.

The unperceived war which Germany thus waged was far more potential with the reduction of mankind than her military war. By the savagery of her armies she brought upon the regions she invaded devastations that can never be adequately told or imagined. But what was far worse, she infected her enemies with her own

military mentality. By her psychic savagery,—a savagery so subtle and Satanic that the sane national mind
may not conceive of it,—she had penetrated the world
before the war began. And it was by this science or
metaphysic of influence that Germany was able to use
unnumbered agents and agencies which were unconscious
of their assidious service.

Most of the peace societies, for example, were, during
the war, in the service of Germany—some of them consciously, some unconsciously. Switzerland was crowded
with representatives of different pacifist organizations
working unremittingly for a German peace. Various
religious societies, both Catholic and Protestant, pam-
phleteered Switzerland on behalf of a peace that should
accord with the pan-German purpose. Their chief business—which business was unconsciously carried on by
good but undiscerning men—was to break down the dis-
tinction between the morality of the German politic and
that which was at least professed by her opponents.

Then the universities and schools of the Allied nations
had become an especial channel for the communication of
Germanism. Prior to the war, Germany had succeeded
in thoroughly establishing the legend of her superior
scholarship. Belief in German intellectual pre-eminence
was universally prevalent. In England and America,
this superiority and pre-eminence were taken for granted.
A German diploma or degree was a first condition of a
collegiate or university position of any importance.
And, preparatory to that, was the fact that our American
common school system was founded precisely upon the
Prussian model.

It is well to pause here a moment and consider this
model. There is no better example of Germanism than
the educational system upon which the State based its
perpetuity and imperial increase. German education
had been made a primary branch of Prussian militarism.
In no true sense could the German schoolmasters be
called educators: they were the drill-sergeants by whom
the children of the people were herded and disciplined
for docility and obedience to the State. Their pedagogy
provided a method, it is true, but a method that was an

assault upon the soul of the child from the days of infancy till maturity was attained; a method, too, that rendered both democracy and individuality psychologically impossible.

The superiority of the German educational system was a part of a well-nigh universal academic delusion. Instead of being superior, the German intellect was inferior in all that pertained to a true human culture, in all that pertained to either mental or moral comprehension. Its distinctive mark had been the totality of its intellectual and moral indefiniteness, its ignorance of essential intellectual integrity. The German intellect was that of a highly-trained animal, sharpened to material and military uses, but with an activity outside the realm of moral comprehension and motivity. Even when evolving its prodigious fogs of philosophy, it had all the unmorality, the unhumanity, of primitive man. As examples, only a German Fichte could glorify Machiavelli as a true disciple of Christ: no Italian ever did it.

No, the German mentality and its processes were not enlightening the world; rather, with their persistent and unclean penetrative power, they were darkening and debasing it. Nor do we yet perceive the power and the persistence of that penetration, how it is to-day shaping the mentality of the world. So far as the German mind is concerned, it has not been conquered, it is rather the victor over the nations. In all that essentially counts, the governmental mind of mankind has become German: it is Germany that has won the war—so much so that the public schools of America are to-day more Prussian than the schools of Germany.

XII

Nothing could have been more favorable, in every worldly sense, than the situation of Germany at the beginning of the year 1914. Intellectually and commercially, she was encircling and permeating the globe. If she had not gone to war, in a decade or two her possession of the world would have been achieved without the firing of a gun; and the possession would have been absolute. She had but to go on, even unto the reaping of the harvest she had sown. She was manufacturing each year more of the things which England consumed; she was taking British trade from British colonies, and pushing British shipping from British ports; she was making the mind of Oxford and directing the education of America; Russia was becoming a German commercial colony; Asia Minor and the Turkish Empire would soon have become hers; she had nothing to fear from France, and she had economically occupied Italy. In a little while, her efficiency would have become the desire of all nations; she was setting all the industrial as well as intellectual fashions.

Even by now, had she not gone to war, we should be dwelling in a world largely German-minded. No madness so suicidal ever possessed a people as that which precipitated the Germans into the war. Of war they had no need, but rather the utter need of avoiding it. They were in the certain way of accomplishing all their ends without the mobilization of a soldier. And there is no accounting for this madness except upon the assumption that the Germany that then was had to be destroyed. It was as if God decreed the Prussian destruction in order to give our civilization its last chance to repent and to redeem itself. It was better to risk the ruin of the world than that it should continue in the Prussian course. Better a world reduced to its primal elements, better that God begin creation anew, than that the Prussian mind should procure its conscript world. Yea, it were better that the world perish utterly than that the Prussian should form it into his image. ·

XIII

For it was the spiritual existence of humanity that was at stake—for this that God ran the last risk as regards our civilization. It was for this that God willed, if we may so phrase it, Germany's destruction. For Germany was more than a geographical or political or national entity; Germany was a state of mind—a state of mind in which spirit had become wholly subject to matter.

Indeed, this was what the war was about and all that it was about—shall spirit serve matter or matter serve spirit? Shall spiritual forces be subjected to material efficiency? Or shall the material world be plastic and subject to spirit?

Matter determined upon making spirit its servant —that was Germany in 1914: it is England, France and America now. Spirit determined upon making matter its divine image and the instrument of its perfect freedom—that was the America that was vocal in Wilson in 1917.

Nor is this issue between matter and spirit only what the war was about: it is what the world is about. It is the final meaning of man, the reason and justification of his being.

XIV

Germany was on the side of matter. She was against the Imminent Spirit striving for the plasticity of matter and for the creation of a world that, in every atom and action, and in its achieved totality, shall be but one image and organization of the Christ. And for the fight she fought, and for the mind that moved all her forces of whatever sort, she must repent. Until she repents, she goes down the ways of death, dragging the world with her.

But should Germany repent, should she change her mind about the meaning of man and of nations, should hence some Christly conception of power come upon her, then to-morrow she might lead the world as high as she has to-day brought it low. The peoples that so long held the whole world at bay, that easily would have possessed themselves of the world if they had had able and noble chieftains, these peoples have capacities the world needs—that the world cannot do without. They are potential with a power to work a redemption that shall over-pay the ruin they have wrought. As great as was their ability to work evil, so great is their ability to work good. Would they be seized by the passion to become servants of humanity instead of its lords, would they change their psychic war for dominion into spiritual contribution, they might yet heal the nations stricken through their madness—yea, even lead them under the law of the Lamb that Sitteth Upon the Throne. Let the German's powers of organization, the German's general efficiency, be laid consecrate upon the altar of humanity, and the super-humanity that he evilly dreamed may be changed into a super-humanity become the realization of The Dream Divine. It is now possible for the Germany that wrought so great a wrong to work a righteousness that shall infinitely out-measure the wrong. And Germany's redemptive possibility is Germany's imperious responsibility—mayhap Germany's last chance.

XV

Nor is it only the German who must repent and be forgiven: we must all equally repent. Germany's need of repentance and forgiveness has passed unto all nations: for Germany has conquered them. Germany has conquered the world—conquered it spiritually and phychically, mentally and morally—conquered it in the things that really matter. Germany's pre-war system of espionage has become the basis of America's national administration of justice. The militarism of Germany has mastered the governmental motivity and procedure of France. The imperialistic purpose of Germany must be looked for in the swollen super-imperialism of Great Britain. The state policy of Germany, so infidel to every element of faith or honor between nations and men, has become the moral order of the human commonality.

And whereas Germany might claim consideration because of her immemorial training in dishonor, because her very pietism and mysticism were all sphered around the idea of the divineness of sheer might, we who were associated in war against her are without excuse. We have sinned against the light—the light which we had, or professed to have, and which Germany neither had nor professed to have. Germany's war, too, at least in its origins, confessedly had world-dominion for its purpose, and frankly proclaimed German superiority as its warrant. But upon our banners were blazoned all the catchwords of democracy, of public justice in Europe, of self-determination for every people, of an actual society of free and federate nations.

Germany sinned according to her faith; she had taken our declared evil to be her declared good. But we who flaunted our antipodal principles upon all the world's winds, we have been infidel to all our earlier inspirations, to all our high professions, to all the motives whereby we mobilized our peoples. We are endeavoring to lay the new foundations of the world in a supreme lie. We have converted Germany's most horrible sins into our own moral complacency. We have predicated the progress of mankind, so far as we have to do with it, upon a super-hypocrisy so brazen, so phenomenal, that it might well shame the stars from their courses, and blot their light from the eyes of man.

And never did the German peoples themselves believe the evil of us that we have done. Burdened as they are with their yet unacknowledged guilt, disintegrating and bewildered and not knowing what to do, denied even the right to repent if they would, their expectations shattered by our prodigious apostacy, by our gross yet gay infidelity to every principle for which we professed to make war, they even yet await some redemptive gestures from the Anglo-Saxon nations—Italy alone has made the divine gesture.

Nor only of our infidelities must we repent, nor only for our sins seek forgiveness: we must repent of our infinitely worse righteousness. We must pass from the monstrous mechanics of an archaic justice, imposturous and performing always for masters and never for men, into the light and under the law and the justice of love. In this justice only,—the justice procured by forgiveness, —is the sole power able to lift the curse to-day consuming the world.

VI.

IN THE LIGHT OF THE LONDON CONFERENCE.

What is the other plan? The traditional one of crushing the enemy, so that he can't begin again, and leaving the matter there. To men who have little knowledge of history, strong passions, and a desire to win for the sake of winning, this plan seems to be beyond question the only one. The position, as they see it, is very simple. "Germany made the war, gratuitously and unprovoked. Put it out of her power to do it again, and there will not be another war." But this simple view leaves out almost the whole of the facts. In the first place, Germany did not make the war gratuitously and unprovoked. It was not a peaceful Europe upon which she sprang it; it was the Europe of armed anarchy on which I have dwelt. That is the essential fact. The relative responsibility of different States, during the ten years of diplomacy preceding the war, though not unimportant, is secondary. I cannot here digress into the question of how that responsibility should be distributed. I have discussed it at length in another place. But if we remember that there were wars before Germany was united, wars in which no German State took part, wars in which the British fought on the side of German States, wars in which the menace of "domination" came not from Germans, but from Frenchmen or Russians, we shall see at once that the causes of war go far deeper and are far more complex than the ambition of any particular State. It follows that the cure for war must go deeper than the reduction of one State to impotence.

G. Lowes Dickinson.

VI

IN THE LIGHT OF THE LONDON CONFERENCE

I.

THE gods have rung up the curtain on the third act of the world-tragedy. The London scene of yesterday may prove the most woeful moment for mankind since the armies of the Kaiser crossed the Belgian frontier. No man can foresee what greater and worse wastes of life, what ultimate agonies and sorrows, what conclusive despairs, will disclose themselves upon this planetary stage, ere the curtain comes down. It is as if the life of man upon the earth was now released to sheer fate; as if the reins of human destiny were at last tossed to maddest chance. And this at the hands of the men we conveniently call statesmen—the men who have made themselves keepers of the nations; who have ostensibly charged themselves with the responsibility of procuring peace for the peoples. Nor is it merely their incredible callousness and baseness, their stark treasons and perjuries, that so bemazes the peoples and renders them impotent to act; it is the revelation of a stupidity, both moral and intellectual, that parallels even the cupidity and duplicity. It is the total lack of brains, of any sort of adequacy, as well as the absence of all apprehension and pity and prescience, that denotes the London Conference as the dark opening scene of a new stage in the world-tragedy—a new descent of man down the Tartarian steeps.

And this new stage has been set by the Parisian Junta that imposes itself upon the world as France—the France that compassed the deception and destruction of Wilson; the France that achieved her peace of loot and revenge; the France that, seeking a dead Germany, would yet somehow make the dead Germany a perennial living tributary; the France that would make the kingdoms and peoples of continental Europe her military satrapies; the France that has armed Poland and Hungary and Rumania for a new and early war against Russia, and that is meanwhile subsidizing new Russian revolutions. It is the France that would not and will not let the world have peace in which to recover and live, or even peace wherein to die. It is the France whose agents, military, diplomatic and financial, have at every point in Europe and Asia and Africa, and from the day of the Armistice till now, striven and plotted against reconciliation among nations and good will among men. *It is the France whom Germany has conquered: for the belief that France has conquered Germany is legend and nothing more: Germany has conquered France utterly.. In the light of the actual and the essential, the victory of Foch is a tale for the nursery histories that supply our common schools.. It is the mind of Germany that is marching on through French propaganda and military adventure. What yesterday was Prussian is today the soul of France. And not by coercion; for France dwells eagerly and voraciously, of her own free and wilful choice, in complete captivity to the Prussian purpose, the Prussian spirit.*

II.

It is a mere waste of time and patience to discuss the London Conference in moral terms. It was an occasion as unmoral, in fact, as far removed from sense or question of right or wrong, justice or injustice, as the sirocco of Sahara or the scream of the hyena in the desert night. The essence of the conference was the struggle of France for a pretext for the occupation of Germany. Britain yielded, finally, in the hope of having done with the French bother, and of thereby being better able to carry on her own imperial appropriations of Asia.

It is true, the Italians fought hard against the application of the sanctions. The man who incarnated what was left of moral sense or dignity in the Supreme Council—the man who indeed rose head and shoulders above the other Allied representatives—Count

Sforza, of Italy, strove mightily in the background for a policy of reconciliation and against the French program. Yet, because of the economic dependence of Italy, Sforza and his worthy colleagues were forced to give their ashamed and indignant consent.

As far as the French were concerned, the conclusion of the conference was pre-arranged. No one would insult the French representatives by believing that they expected the amount fixed at the Paris Conference to be paid by the Germans. These are astronomical and not terrestrial figures—figures to be mobilized for the measurements of the stars and the spaces, but figures beyond the facts and finances of our little earth. The sums named at Paris were never meant to be taken seriously except by the stupid international public. The purpose of Paris was to name an amount so high, and to lay down conditions so drastic, that their inapplicability and the consequent German rejection of them would provide pretext for the long-prepared French invasion of Germany.

The British knew this very well—though in the end they yielded abjectly, and the British prime minister became the French spokesman. As the *Daily News* of London put it, "Mr. Lloyd George brushed aside the solid offers of a peaceful solution put forward by the German delegates, and committed the Entente to the gravest decision taken since the Armistice. There is not a single intelligent student of the reparation problem who will not recognize in this hopeless and barren speech a complete capitulation to France. It represents, in fact, the triumph at last of the French policy of revenge and all the sinister implications that it contains. It is scarcely surprising that the British prime minister said not a word in legal justification of the application of force, for it is legally indefensible. On moral grounds, what is there to be said for it? The Allies are to invade Germany to enforce the terms of a treaty which they have themselves discarded. They refuse to give even the most cursory examination to a proposition which meets, for the first five years, at least, all demands."

III.

So the march to Berlin has begun. The Parisian Junta, having previously penetrated and corrupted the whole of Europe, has achieved its initial purpose. Assembled behind the prestige of Marchal Foch (whose knowledge of economics and politics scarcely exceeds that of a child of four) the Junta bestrides the Continent. Before the vision of this Junta looms a South Germany linked with Austria and Hungary under the Hapsburg crown, the whole administered as an essential French protectorate. The same vision joins to this confederation that monstrous French imposture of a restored Polish nationality. In the same evil vision Rumania is bound to a French Poland and a French Hungary in an early advance against Russia. A Romanoff Russia, financed and exploited and directed from Paris, completes the black Apocalypse.

Such is the precise program of the politico-financial group which governs France—the profiteers, who, by underground means during the war, furnished the Germans with munition materials wherewith to kill Frenchmen; the men who have capitalized the bones of their country's sacred dead, and who have made merchandise of the miseries of devastated France in all the markets of the world.

Yet blinder men have never been, and never has power been more blindly wielded. For whatever happens now, Briand and the Junta he serves have signed the death-warrant of France. Everyone who loves France, everyone who has militantly defended the French cause (as the writer of these words has done), will weep over the ruin the French rulers have wrought. The farther France now marches upon her program, the deeper will be the perdition upon which she enters.

IV.

It is possible, of course, that within a week or two the Germans will make new propositions—propositions so conciliatory, so obviously the extreme of what Germany can do, that England and Italy will demand their acceptance.

Even so, the masters of France will not take their teeth out of the body of Germany.

Keep this fact steadily in mind: *the keepers of France do not want Germany to make a satisfactory reparation.* What they actually want is a pretext for the indefinite occupation and exploitation of Germany. Even if the Germans satisfy the very last demand of the French Government, France will henceforth give Germany no peace, no chance to recover. France wishes to demonstrate to the world that Germany cannot be safely left at large except under French dominion.

Indeed, the whole French program in Germany, in Europe, in Asia, is not for peace anywhere or in any particular, but for war and conquest everywhere and in every particular.

Or it is possible that Germany will settle down into an indefinite non-resistance of the French occupation. There are not a few of the ablest men of Germany who urgently counsel this resolution and procedure. They feel assured in their own minds that this is the way to a victory more complete than ever the Prussian armies could have won. They know perfectly well that France cannot continue an occupation indefinitely without her own national bankruptcy ensuing. They know that the French government has no money wherewith to continue such occupation. They also know that, though the population of France is the richest on the Continent, yet the possessors of French wealth have always escaped taxation; nor will they now pay the taxes that might save their country from national bankruptcy. The Germans further know that England cannot and that America will not furnish more money to France. The German tactic may therefore be to let France exhaust herself in her scheme of occupation and administration.

Moreover, the Germans know well enough a monstrous fact carefully concealed from the English and the American public. That is, that *the enormous French deficit and threatened bankruptcy are not due to the money France has spent and must yet spend in restoring the devasted regions. The deficit is due to the French military career of the last two years: to the subsidization of continued invasions of Russia;* to the maintenance of Polish armies—for the being of which there is no excuse; to the military occupation of Hungary—now bursting with French munitions; to the wicked and utterly indefensible conquest of Syria— whose Lebanon people are more capable of self-government than the Poles or the Serbs or even the citizens of Paris; to the conscription and maintenance of the millioned black hordes of French Africa; these are the sources of the French deficit, these are the places where the money of France has gone. And that Germany must justly be made pay for the immense ruin she has wrought does not in the least change the fact that the restoration of these ruined regions is not the cause of French bankruptcy. The cause is, as I have said, the vast and varied military adventures of France since peace was supposed to have been made.

<h2 style="text-align:center">V.</h2>

It may be that the British, seeing the incorrigibility of Paris, have finally though secretly decided to let France go her own way unto her own doom. There is no doubt that England would like to be relieved of France. The drag of France upon the British neck is becoming practically insupportable. The British probably foresee that if France marches to Berlin, and at the same time sends her military missions to lead Poland and Hungary and Rumania against Russia, the French missions and armies may never return to Paris, or return only in fragments. With France thus disatrously occupied on the Continent, England can have Western Asia to herself. France has been a continual block in the wheel of the British imperial program since the Armistice was signed. That France has everywhere intrigued against England, that France has always been faithless to her Allies—of this the British foreign office is perfectly aware. Thus there is the possibility that not only Germany, but Great Britain as well, has decided that the best way to deal with France now is to let the Parisian Junta have its way. And, meanwhile, through the gates of Hamburg and Bremen, Great Britain will have come to satisfactory if tacit commercial arrangements with Germany, and not much of worth be left for either France or America.

VI.

But there is a more direful and even probable consequence to be considered. It is this—that a military dictatorship will rise in Russia with Trotsky as dictator and with Lenin eliminated; and that this thoroughly militarized Russia will come to terms with the industrial magnates of Berlin and the Junkers of Prussia. Germany may feel driven to this as her last hope of self-preservation. If that military dictatorship triumphantly arise, then the fabled and French Poland will quickly dissolve before the Russian advance, and Russia and Germany will march together toward the Rhine. Stricken Austria will revive as a state of the German Empire, and amid the whole convulsion engulfing Europe and bringing woe upon America, the catastrophe of western civilization will be complete.

Mayhap it needs to be so. Mayhap not even the heart of God could do more with a civilization so materially minded as ours, so lost to truth and faith, and with leaders so sodden in corruption, so imbecile in decision and action, as those that now direct the destinies of the dying nations.

VII.

Now all this has a profoundly penetrative and predestinative effect upon the choices and destinies of America. The French have been clever enough in their calculations as to the effect of the London rupture with Germany upon American public opinion and diplomatic action. By so maneuvering as to mask their determination to prevent a settlement with Germany with the appearance of urgent efforts to force a settlement, the French politicians have accomplished two things highly desirable to them and their financial masters. The first is, that of placing the American Government in so awkward a position toward Germany that the projected separate peace according to the Knox Resolution must be postponed. Second, under the crafty guidance of that bombastic apostate, Mr. Viviani, an avalanchian propaganda for France will be carried on in America. The first sweeping advance of this propaganda is already far under way. It is camouflaged by a vehement bestirring of public opinion against a hypothetical pro-German propaganda in the United States. The American public is now made to believe that a profound and pervasive pro-German campaign is imperiling America's national integrity.

Now this proclaimed pro-German propaganda is nothing else under the sun than the prelude of an actual and exceedingly corrupt French propaganda, financed by certain international gambling institutions known as banks and operating between New York and Paris. The shabbiest foreign schemes of certain New York financial groups are carried on through Parisian banking houses. Parisian, for the reason that the standard of honor required in the American financial institutions, such as it is, has no existence in the like financial institutions of Paris. The soul of French finance is its corruptive power; and the favor in which it is held by certain American financiers is due to the convenience it affords for corruptly procuring concessions and for the carrying on of speculations that cannot possibly be procured or proceed through American or English banks directly. *Moreover, this crafty prevention of an American peace with Germany, this intensively cultivated French propaganda in our midst, mobilizing as it does the blind nationalism of young Americans to its standard, is not only destructive to an American knowledge of the truth; it is distinctly destructive to American commerce as well. That commerce with Germany and with Russia which American industry sorely needs at the present time, and which would decidedly advantage American labor just now, is blocked by the*

French consecration of our stupidity in dealing with both Germany and Russia. The American manufacturer and business man, despite his supposed competence and enlightened self-interest, is being calamitously duped by the Parisian Junta.

Nor only today; for well on to two years, now, the international policy of our American State Department has been increasingly directed by the French foreign office—which foreign office at least has the merit of having pursued one consistent evil policy from the days of Louis XI till the days of President Harding. And the consequence of this unconscious and even servile subservience of our American foreign policy to that of France is the cutting off of America from what ought to be her redemptive industrial relation to Europe, her both profitable and beneficent relation to the whole planet. We are being seduced by France into a national state of mind, into a diplomatic conduct, that can have no other result than that of rendering both our commerce and our friendship with the nations of the world perditionable.

VIII.

The writer can be accused of no pro-German tendencies or preferences. For years before the war he sought to arouse public opinion in Europe and in America, to the limited extent to which he could reach that opinion, against the Prussian purpose and its peril to civilization. But the peril that was Prussian has now passed to the French financiers and politicians. It is these who are seeking, both overtly and covertly, by intrigue and by war, to restore a medieval and monarchical Europe; to subject the nations unto the will and the profit of the French concessionnaire; and to destroy the last vestige of honesty, the last hope of democracy, the last basis for co-operation and good will among men. And it is against these that every believer in democracy, every advocate of honor and faith between nations, every lover not only of humanity as a whole but of the French people as well, should today and at all cost take his stand.

VII.
THE TREASON OF FRANCE.

Further, even if it were true that the present war had been caused exclusively by German aggression, it would not follow that by crushing Germany we would obtain a permanently secured peace against her. Let us turn to history. For twenty years Europe fought France, as the Power menacing the liberties of all other States. France, in fact, did succeed, as Germany has not, in conquering and incorporating with herself a great part of Europe. The force she developed, relatively to that of her enemies, was incomparably greater than that which Germany has shown. After almost continuous war for twenty years she was beaten, beaten to her knees, and her capital occupied in triumph. Did she thereafter cease to be a menace? On the contrary. During a great part of the nineteenth century the ambition of France was still the bugbear of Europe, and especially of England. Every internal revolution in her government was expected to unchain a war either of liberty or of domination. She was the firebrand of the world, or so believed to be, and was so far from being reduced to impotence by all she had suffered that she could still think herself, even up to 1870, invincible. 1871 appeared to have annihilated her. Did it? Look at her now!

G. LOWES DICKINSON.

Those who base their reading of the traditional permanent France upon the observation of our own lifetime take too short a view. It may be the period from 1870 to 1906, or thereabouts (when the Millerand-Poincare school began to win its way), which was abnormal—the period of calm, and concentration, and relative isolation. What has happened with victory is, on this reading, not a momentary nervous disturbance, but a reversion to type, the re-emergence of a half-buried, subconscious, but very persistent personality. France is herself again. It was seldom a meek or unagressive self. The picture in the Premier's memorandum of a martyr France, "invaded four times in 120 years," verges on comedy. On the three earlier occasions the invasion was but the backwash of a violent outward rush. Was the France of Leipzig and Waterloo unaggressive, or was the Man of Destiny a man of peace? National character is made—who shall say in what proportions?—by historical tradition and economic forces. Both tend in France to militarism. The rather backward small-scale industry, the relatively slight commercial enterprise, the clinging to inheritances and investments, cause the French to hug their claims on Germany and Russia as we do not. It is the very stability of this society, based on thrift and inheritance, with its emphasis on keeping rather than on making, which renders it so implacable in the matter of debt. Its military power is its chief asset. The colored armies and the submarines are to levy tribute for it, much as mills, and forges, and ships make profit for Englishmen, Germans, or Americans.

THE NATION & THE ATHENAEUM, LONDON.

VII

THE TREASON OF FRANCE

I.

In the fervor wherewith we rushed to the defence of France and to the turning back of the German, in 1914, we forgot much of our history. We failed to remember how many of the wars of Germany, from the time of the Ceasars down to Napoleon, had been defensive wars. We also forgot the wrongs which Germany suffered at the hands of France, for more than two centuries, and the wide waste and deep woe which came to all the German states from Napoleon. We forgot, too, that France had always either held or sought military dominion over Europe, and that her historic policy had been one of political and economic destruction: she had always sought the disunion and disintegration of other peoples. Whenever there has been an exception to this, it has been a case of upholding a foreign tyranny which she could use for her own ends—as in the case of Russia. The Czars would long ago have ceased to be, and a more desirable revolution in Russia long ago have taken place, had it not been for the gold of France.

Nor did we, losing as we did all sense of proportion in view of the German's moral enormity, take account of certain traits of French national and individual character. One of these is that self-esteem, that vanity, which renders France a nation without the sense of gratitude. Whatever you may do for France, whatever another nation may do for France, whatever the world may do for France, will be taken by France as her due, and less than her due. Of gratitude France is yesterday and today and forever destitute.

It is thus that whenever you put power into the hands of France, you arm her against the peace of the world, and for your own destruction. And if you will examine the history of Europe for the last thousand years only, you will not be able to escape the discovery that France has always been, as she is now, the chief enemy to peace and goodwill, to mutual confidence and co-operation, among European peoples.

II.

It requires a degree of hardihood to speak the truth about France—or about anything else, for that matter—at the present time. Since a news service no longer exists, but only propaganda for this interest and that, England and America are perilously ignorant of what is happening to the world, and especially of the evil activities of France since the Armistice. The wrongs that Germany wrought we know, and more than know. Of the wrongs wrought by France we know nothing; and we are in no mood for knowing about them. The Prussian peril was proclaimed before and during the war—and no one proclaimed it more urgently than the writer of these words. Of the French menace we are dangerously ignorant.

Moreover, the difficulty of telling the truth about France—or about the present European situation as a whole—is enhanced by the French creed that France is exempt from criticism. Lloyd George's warning to the French press was wasted, so far as France is concerned. You may criticise Great Britain and the British to your heart's content—more than likely the Britons will applaud you. The least hint of a criticism of France puts you down in the French mind as either a villain or a protector of the Germans. An article by the writer, published in an American journal, in criticism of the conduct of France at the London Conference, is described at length in a Parisian journal as a "hymn of hate." The propositions of Dr. Simons to the London Conference were written down in Paris as "the desperation of scoundrelism." The proposition which many American and English publicists urged—namely, that the reconstruction of the devastated regions be undertaken by German soldiers—was characterised as a wily scheme of the German Government to get German workers "housed in almost luxury." The French were told the Germans would have to have exceptional amusements and privileges, and shorter hours of labour than were allowed to French workers. Thus the French contractors—a member of whose union is M. Loucheur—preserved their profits; preserved them, also, by singing songs of lamentation over criticisms of French policy emanating from America and England.

III.

Today, France is anew filling the world with the cry that she has sacrificed herself for humanity. This was the burden which monsieur Viviani bore on his lips to America. Yet the precise opposite is the truth. Humanity has sacrificed itself for France, and for a France basely ungrateful.. The present evil plight of the world is primarily due to French dominance in the councils of the nations. The nations of Europe are dying of the French plague. And there is no compensating value in France. The France of to-day is not worth the price humanity has already paid, these last six years, for her continued existence.

To French governmental and financial minds, to the historic appetite of the French politicians, the world and all therein exists for France. And these are to-day demanding that the world be organized solely with reference to France's safety—and they are demanding this as her due tribute. The egotism of the French governing class, the sordid harlequinry of her politics, the greedy harlotry of her diplomacy, these have gone beyond even the ancient pseudo-decencies of nations. Indeed, history shows no more forbidding spectacle than that of the French concessionnaires and politicians making merchandise of the bones and shed blood of her dead sons in all the markets of the world. The Shylock's asset which the French diplomats have made of the French dead ought to shock the sensibilities of even our cruel and bemuddled times.

IV.

In order to understand this French attitude, it is best that the stark truth of France's relation to her Allies during the war be starkly stated. Every Foreign Office knows, and every War Office too, and knows down to the last intelligence officer, that throughout the war France was faithless to her Allies, continually intriguing against each from the war's beginning to its end.

Consider America and Wilson. Before America entered the war, and when France still hoped to win without American intervention, she secretly sought to discourage such participation out of fear of Wilson's authority in the Peace Conference. After America was in France, the one absorbing motive of French policy was to discredit Wilson and destroy his program before these should appear at the Peace Table. The writer was in a place to know what France was doing throughout three continents. He knows that the destruction of Wilson and Wilsonism was a responsibility laid upon French agents throughout Europe, Asia and Africa. This was also the consuming purpose of Monsieur Clêmenceau—and a purpose which was completely fulfilled.

Whatever America or the world may to-day think or say about Wilson, and after debiting him with all the faults and failures you please, it still remains true that this man presented to the nations the sole policy that might have procured a new international order; that might have initiated an era of conciliation and goodwill. And he presented his principles in all good faith. He was the one outstanding personality, his idea was the one outstanding worth, of the world-war. That his idea was greater that his ability to execute it in the face of universal treachery and hostility of the governing classes—this is true. But if it had been honestly accepted and intelligently applied, mankind would ere now have been pitched upon a higher plane of progress: we should by this time be dwelling in a world of brave initiative and good promise instead of a world of perdition and despair.

That the world-project of Wilson was not carried out, that general evil instead of good is now our portion, is primarily the work of France. It was France that brought Wilson low, and that, in slaying Wilson, slew the highest hope, the most creative and commanding expectation, that ever beset the nations, and also France that thus caused the death by disease and starvation of unnumbered millions of defenceless children and their mothers. And so the ultimate records of these tremendous days will certainly inscribe it—inscribe against France this mightiest defeat which our common humanity ever suffered—this betrayal, this spiritual reversion, of mankind.

Again,—and this without reference to Great Britain's imperialistic craft or predatory operations,—during the years wherein British soldiers were giving their lives for the defence of French soil, France intrigued against Great Britain in every quarter of the planet.

The same is true of France's hidden conduct towards Italy. Twice, if not thrice, the action of Italy saved France. The early announcement of Italy's neutrality, her refusal to engage in an offensive war at the side of her formal allies, Germany and Austria, enabled France to take her soldiers from her southern frontiers; whence Paris was saved. Again, in the darkest hour of the war, when Russia had fallen and it seemed that victory would be with the German, and when Italy was yet poorly prepared for war, the Italians threw themselves into the breach and thereby again saved France. Yet not only has France been destitute of a single act or impulse of gratitude for the sacrificial service or Italy. She has, behind the scenes, been Italy's continuous and hateful enemy. During the Peace Conference, and up to this present hour, every ill service which France could render Italy has by France been so rendered.

It was France that set her face against Wilson's idea of a free Poland, until she conceived of a Poland armed as a French satrapy and a point of attack against Russia. It was France that intrigued against the Rumania which she would now mobilise against the Soviet Republic. It was France that permited a new slaughter of the

Armenians—the news of which slaughter has been kept from the world—comparable to the slaughter permitted by the Germans; and it is through France that Armenia was again sacrificed to the Turk, even while Monsieur Viviani was ostensibly championing the cause of Armenia for one preposterous day at Geneva. It is in order to satisfy France that Britain has broken faith with her Arab allies, and that the fine and free peoples of Lebanon Syria, as well as the Arabs of Damascus, have been delivered to the French spoiler. And it is France that yesterday filled the press of England and America with news of a preparing Bolshevist invasion of Poland—which news every informed man in Europe knew to be false—in order to cover the war which she herself was then inciting against Russia. France was then bent upon a policy that meant a practical re-opening of the European war. She was arranging an invasion of Russia by Poland, Roumania and Hungary, all under the command of French officers. It was to mask this invasion that she spread abroad the news of a "Red attack" upon Poland.

V.

So, staged and managed by the Parisian Junta, and as pitiless as it is cynical, the devil's lewd comedy of nations continues.

Yesterday, it was in Hungary the scene was laid. But the genesis thereof went back to the middle of the war, and to subsequent intrigues reaching from Paris to Berne. One of the managers of the Hungarian scene was a Hapsburg agent in Switzerland in 1918. And, though France and Austro-Hungary were at war, this Magyar magnate was *persona grata* at Paris, and traveled back and forth with the freedom of a French diplomatic agent. The next preparation for the Hungarian scene was the presence of Bela Kun in Budapest. English and American workers are still obsessed by the notion that Bela Kun represented an uprising of Hungarian Socialists. He represented nothing of the kind—for by his régime the Socialists were exiled, imprisoned, or assassinated. Not by Hungarian Socialists, but by agents of

Parisian concessionnaires, accompanying the French Army of Occupation, was Bela Kun in Budapest for so long a time; and the fabled Soviet régime, deluding Hungarian workers as it did, was a French preparation, first for rich concessions in the Banat, and then for a French conducted return of the Hapsburgs.

VI.

Innumerable indeed are the ways in which the spirit of France is being manifested throughout Europe today —ways without one spark of magnanimity or decency in international relations; without fidelity to a promise. The diplomacy of loot and lies, the fountain whereof is the Parisian Junta, is now supreme in Europe. Any peace made in Europe under the French domination will be purely a peace of plunder.

Even the things which call for some decency, if not chivalry, are not to be found. Take the cynical and brutal violation of the ancient treaties regarding the zones upon which the economic life of Geneva and French Switzerland depend. Or consider an instance like the following, furnished me by a publicist of international authority, who was himself Francophile during the war. "On the occasion of the exposition at Lyons in the early summer of 1914, the municipality of that city requested the trustees of the Goethe Museum in Frankfurt to lend the exhibition committee some objects belonging to that collection. With this request they gladly complied and sent to Lyons a considerable number of objects, among them the original portrait of Goethe painted by Colbe, some statues, silhouettes, manuscripts and the original edition of 'Faust' illustrated by Delacroix. The Grand Duke of Weimar lent for the same purpose his special set of the great Weimar edition of the works of Goethe. In the meantime the war broke out, and the exhibits were kept back in France. All endeavors on the part of Professor Dr. Heuer, the chief conservator of the Goethe Museum, to get back the treasures thus loaned through the mediation of neutral savants, proved ineffectual. Professor Heuer addressed himself directly to President

Millerand, pleading that there are things which ought to be considered as being beyond the strifes of nations, such as relics of great poets and thinkers, like Dante, Shakespeare, Goethe or Molière. To this President Millerand replied that he had passed the letter on to the Minister of Foreign Affairs. Now the news has come from France that the French Government refuses to restore the objects in question."

VII.

Nor is there aught of good report to set over against the treason of France. Not one magnanimous movement, not one generous gesture or action, not one disinterested proposal, not one syllable of reconciliation or good-will, has come from the French diplomats or politicians. Not one good thing for humanity has come out of France since she signed the contract she never meant to keep with Germany. There has come only one continuous and inclusive war against peace, against international understanding, against every approach to brotherhood, against every general human good. Avarice—avarice winged with revenge—has been the soul of French policy; and it is an avarice without shame or pity, an avarice without faith in any good human action or impulse.

And this avarice of France has slain its millions where the German armies slew their hundreds. We Anglo-Saxons would understand this, if once we threw into our perspective the piteous peoples that have met miserable death, or disease worse than death, through the blockades France procured; through the French peace imposed upon Austria; through the French policy towards Russia—which policy both England and America have followed.

VIII.

It is our misfortune that the accepted reports of the war and the peace have so warped our powers of perception, have provided us with such false angles of vision, have so stultified our capacity for moral discernment and measurement, that the events of these terrible years, as we see them, are monstrously misproportioned to each other or to reality. For instance, the German devastation of France and Belgium, and their accompanying cruelties, are obvious and objective. They held the eye and the attention, and can be measurably estimated. They are also to some degree intelligible, when once we make allowance for the fact that war in itself is always and everywhere an atrocity, always and everywhere savage and vile and lawless. But to any mind capable of seeing things in their right proportions, and of forming rational moral judgments, the German atrocities in France and Belgium are but incidental when compared with the illegal and pitiless economic warfare of the Entente against the womanhood and childhood of Europe east of the Rhine—the warfare of the blockades. History will inscribe the essentially French destruction of the Austrian people by starvation as a crime and a cruelty outmeasuring in its guilt and its wantonness the German cruelties in French and Belgian territories. The German atrocities were acts of war—unspeakably abominable acts certainly—but the economic war of the Entente against the womanhood and childhood of the greater part of Europe has been carried on under the cover of the terms of peace—has been carried on perjuriously and lawlessly; and it has been a warfare so stealthy and filthy, so venomous and wanton and cruel, as to be uncharacterisable and indescribable by mortal language. And the very bigness and diabolism of it all, with unnumbered millions dead and a million dying daily, baffles both feeling and imagination.

Charge the Germans with their worst; spare neither German ruler nor soldier nor citizen; exact the uttermost farthing of reparation; yet, before the ultimate assizes of history, this German worst will be found paltry when set beside the insensate cruelty, the illimitable wastes of human life, the infinite perpetrations of human misery, into which the victors in the war have been seduced or coerced by the French Foreign Office.

IX.

It is time that we began to see the things of the war, and the tortures inflicted upon the peoples by the monstrous peace and its makers, in their true proportions. It is time that we began to beware of the yet worse betrayals of humanity into which we may be led by the same French greed that is plunging Europe and Asia into misery and savagery. It would be well if English-speaking peoples—Americans especially—would once more read Mark Twain's satirical yet profound analysis of French national character and the ancient avarice the predicates French national policy. He typifies it in the action of France regarding the taxation of Joan of Arc's native village of Domremy. France made an asset of Joan of Arc at the beginning of the war—just as she is now making an asset of Napoleon. When the wretched King Charles asked Joan of Arc what she would have for herself in return for the service of saving France, she asked only that the people of her peasant village be evermore exempt from taxation. This, and nothing more, should be her reward; and the King and the attendant nobles pledged France to the fulfilment of this request. But thrifty France, which releases her political millionaires from taxation and submits to being governed by the profiteers—by the profiteers who indirectly furnished munition materials to the Germans in order that they might kill Frenchman during the war—long ago broke the pledge to her bannered saint: France continued taxing, to the limit of their capacity, the peasants of Domremy.

X.

France is plotting a monarchist restoration throughout Europe. France is sacrificing the armies of her satrapies for the restoration of the Romanoffs in Russia. France is still stuffing Hungary with arms and munitions for the restoration of the Hapsburgs in Budapest and Vienna. France is intriguing throughout South Germany for the restoration of the Wittelsbachs in Munich, and for a reactionary and submissive Germany. The reactionaries of France are only biding the moment for a *coup d'état* and the restoration of the Bourbon dynasty in Paris.

In order to understand this, one must have made some study of the qualities and conditions of French government. France is governed, as I have already implied, by a Junta of peculiarly corrupt financiers, operating through groups of peculiarly corrupt politicians. These groups are made up of political mandarins, or else political climbers who have achieved the favor of the madarins. There is never any actual change in French politics, in the French government. There is only a perpetual Punch and Judy show before the eyes of the people, behind which show the real government of France by corruption proceeds. Punch comes in and Judy goes out—one French government. Judy comes in and Punch goes out—another French government. But the same speculators and concessionnaires pull the strings of both Punch and Judy. Not that the French government represents the French people: it merely dupes and dazzles them—and takes them to market.

Now this government of France by corruption, tainting everything it touches, has laid infectious hands upon the whole of Europe, of western Asia as well, since the signing of the Armistice; and the money that France is today spending in propaganda in America will have no other result than that of corrupting American vision, American sense of proportion, and of destroying that power of sympathy and understanding, that generosity of attitude, which is native to Americans, in herited from their frontier fathers.

For Monsieur Viviani went to America as a bearer of plague to an already diseased if not dying democracy. Ostensibly, he presented the felicitations of the French Government to President Harding. Actually, he sought to hitch American international policies and proceedings to the French Foreign Office. He went also to precipitate, to intensively cultivate, the French propaganda that was already well under way—masquerading as a revival of Americanism in a campaign against pro-Germanism.

XI.

But there hides another and worse peril in the French propaganda in America—Viviani and Lauzanne following Tradieu; Marshall Foch following Viviani; and Millerand minded to follow Foch. That worst peril is the widening of the breach between America and England. It is a crafty and covert French policy to keep America and England apart, and to prevent a working union of the peoples we accommodatively call Anglo-Saxon. And the increasing cleavage between America and England is the worst peril that has ever beset the family of nations; while an eventual war between America and Britain would be the world's veritable end —the end of all that makes the world's continuance worth while.

Now I am among those who hoped and labored during the war, each according to his large or small place, for some kind of federation or co-operation of the English-speaking peoples. From the beginning of the war I believed, and I still believe, that in this union lies the sole hope of preserving what the human race has gained up till now, or of achieving in the future any sort of democratic internationalism. The union need not be formal, but it must be actual and effectual. If the English-speaking peoples elect to will and to work together for a free and democratic world-order, the human future holds somewhat of promise. If evil interests succeed in putting division and war between the English-speaking peoples, then the way of mankind leads back to the jungle.

I grant you anything you please about the traditional Albion perfidy. I agree with you that what England has lately done in Ireland is more reprehensible, both from the standpoint of law and morals, than what Germany did in Belgium. I will not dispute the long exploitation and economic and civil ruin of India, nor the usurious bleeding of Egypt in the interest of the holders of the atrocious Egyptian bonds. I will not contend with your complaint as to the planetary loot Great Britain has carried off from the war. But, after all the admissions have been made, two things still remain true: first, that the breaking up of the British Empire, at the present time means universal chaos, second that the transmutation of that Empire into a vast commonwealth of free peoples is the surest hope of the preservation of existing world-values for a long time to come. And the initiaion of that commonwealth rests with the United States of America.

It is not the weal of America, nor is it the weal of the world, that they work who seek to put contention and war between American and the peoples that constitute Great Britain: it is rather the final debacle of he world. The forces that are cleaving the breach between England and America to-day are as wicked as any forces that have ever wrought the woe of humanity. And it is this final woe, universally calamitous in its consequences, that the French propaganda is covertly working in the American mind at the present hour. Would that there were some in places of authority who had the sense to see it—to see it before it is too late!

Nor is this a matter that concerns English-speaking peoples alone. Italy, twice irreparably sacrificing herself to save France from the Germans, and betrayed by France without stint or conscience, places her hope for the world's future in the so-called Anglo-Saxon peoples, and prays for a welcome among them. I venture to say that Germany would to-day both humbly and happily co-operate with an English-speaking commonwealth of nations, if she were honorably and honestly permitted so to do.

XII.

The writer of these words is among those who protested to President Wilson against the Armistice, believing that peace, to be magnanimous as well as swift and radical, should be made in Berlin. But he also believed that when America and the Entente covenanted to make peace on the terms of the Fourteen Points, they should keep their sacredly plighted word.

They did not keep their word. The Peace of Versailles, constituted in perjury, in avarice and revenge, is an embodiment of the very soul of planetary evil, a veritable devil's charter. Thus Germany, the criminal and the accused, stands justly in the place of the accuser of the criminals; while the whole pitiful world is repenting in madness and misery, in the daily death of a million mothers and children by starvation, in a world wherein no people any longer trusts another people, no man any longer trusts another man. *And this Peace of Versailles, this devil's world-charter, converting Europe into a snake-pit and laying a deep curse upon the mind of America—this is the creation, not of the French people, but of the Parisian Junta which wrought the destruction of Wilson and of the only program by which the world could have had peace and a higher plane of development. It is this Junta which has smitten the fair lands of France with darkness and her good peoples with blindness, and which is to-day dragging the whole family of man down to long perdition. And so the place of those who perceived the Prussian peril and withstood it—the place of every true lover of France indeed—is now over a-gainst the French peril and in the withstanding of that. It is time that we Anglo-Saxons, first of all, should per-ceive whither the French propaganda is leading us, ere we be impressed into policies and procedures that will issue not only in our own ultimate ruin, but in the ruin of the last hope of our civilization.*

Yea, the France that M. Viviani represented at the White House, the France that is still bestirring American public opinion anew against the dangers of a fabled pro-German propaganda, is the France that is but augmenting the world-ruin which Prussia began. The material de-vastations of France by the Germans, appalling as they were, are indeed trifling, as far as their evil results are concerned, as compared with the moral devastations of France by the French financiers themselves. And France, moreover, now openly fights—and fights with all the wea-pons in the arsenal of the powers of evil—for the con-tinued government of the world by fraud and violence. It is the France that stands, as no modern power except Prussia has stood, against every approach of that peace and good will which go forth from Christ for the healing of the nations.

VIII.
THE BURDEN OF AMERICA

Long, too long America,
Travelling roads all even and peaceful you learn'd from joys
    and prosperity only.
But now, Ah now, to learn from crises of anguish, advancing,
    grappling with direct fate and recoiling not.

Walt Whitman.

The life-destroying ill of humanity at the present day is the
want of a common faith, a common thought, accepted and admitted by all men, which shall relink earth to heaven, the universe to God. Deprived of this common faith, man has bowed
down before lifeless matter, and become a worshipper of the
idol *Self-Interest*. And the first priests of that fatal worship
were kings, princes and evil governments.

Joseph Mazzini.

Let us approach the idea of the League of Nations with confidence. The idea is good and feasible; it is of ideal and practical value. With the former methods of politics no individual
nation can advance any further, nor can humanity. Machiavellism
has done its hideous worst in this war—the system of the
boundless individualistic national life is bankrupt. The nations
realize now that the accentuation of the spirit of self-interest is
fatal to the spirit of community; they are discovering, to their
horror, that they cannot with impunity surrender themselves to a
method whose very essence lies in their liberation from all moral
considerations.
    They are beginning to learn and to value the actual political
force of the moral virtues, and to recognize that without community of spirit there can be no lasting peace, and without the
sacrifice of national egoism no possible solidarity. Each State
will discover, when it comes to examine its war balance, that the
national welfare will in future be identical with the welfare of the
community. The biological conception of national life will give
place to the social conception. The Christian idea of the community of the nations is again abroad in the world, exhorting
the nations to pause and examine their consciences. The future
belongs to Christian democracy.

M. Erzberger.

VIII

THE BURDEN OF AMERICA

I

IN a document addressed to some young Americans starting to the war, in the autumn of 1917, the writer inscribed: "If the German gets the place in the sun he demands, the sun will be blotted out for humanity. In marching against the German, you march to the spiritual rescue of the race. You will be fighting against things more terrible than you dream; you will be fighting for things more splendid than you dream. Go forth holily, candidly confessing your high consecration, and your weapons will turn back powers of darkness, and your armour wing the light that breaks for the healing of the nations."

These words were the writ of an urgent faith; and it was a faith then common to many Americans, caught up by the Great Promise. Absurd they seem now, and indeed childish. For the repudiation of the Promise is complete; to-morrow will but complete the completion. History moves now so rapidly, it is true, that it is impossible to predict far into the future. By the time this confession is in print, some new precipitation may have wrought changes still more unexpected, still more incredible. But this much seems certain: whatever new changes are near, they will not redeem the Promise. The downward steeps will grow steeper, the descent of man swifter and more terrible. Even now, appalling as is the apparent condition of the world, the reality is worse than the appearance. And the evil that now is, with the greater evil to come, fruits naturally from the Conference betrayal of the Promise, after it was ratified and contractually signed by the Powers.

II

Nor do the representatives of the Powers seem capable of learning one lesson, of taking one rational step: they emit no glint of moral reason: they show no sign of historic sense, of economic knowledge, of political capacity. So far as the present hour is concerned, the minds and morals of the Supreme Council are prehistoric. They do but descend from perjury to perjury, from baseness to baseness—until San Remo is reached. There would not seem to be a lower diplomatic level. Yet who knows? Baser depths may be possible to these perfidious dividers of the world. Indeed, the possibility seems to have been realized in London, where the British Prime Minister's negotiations with the Russian ambassador are stressed with the bawdy outbreak of the War Minister against the head of the Russian Government.

The result of it all is, as Dr. Dillon so aptly put it, "we fought to make the world safe for hypocrisy." Whatever one may think of the League of Nations, the League of Lies has been realized; and, so long as the present courtesanship of the professional public informers continues, in these lies the world is inextricably caught. For instance, not one essential thing told abroad about San Remo is true, and not one thing that is true was told abroad. And, taking the tale of these terrible years as a whole, there seems but one thing you may be sure of—whatever you know about The War or The Peace is not true, and whatever is true you do not know.

Really, the globe has become uninhabitable for the truth. The agencies of news have become propaganda agencies of the governments, and the governments are the agencies of the Interests and the Appetites. The peoples have come somewhat to know this—to know that whatever their governments tell them is but for the concealment of either new disasters or new predacities. And the governments, as a result of lying so habitually, are now so entangled in their lies that they can no longer govern.

Nor can the machinery of production produce: capitalism, refusing to face the fact of its increasing incapacity, universally obvious, is no longer able to control the mechanism of its own creation: it has become self-devouring. Meanwhile, one by one the Seven Seals are opening, and the dread pilgrimage of humanity through the deluge of wrath has begun.

III

And all this is a final result of America's failure, in the hour of her divine visitation, to enforce and fulfil the Promise. Be the fault where it will—let it be that Wilson failed his people—let it be that the people failed Wilson—the present abominable state of the world would not have been if America had kept faith with the nations.

There never was but one hope among them: that hope was America. They never believed in their own governments; they never believed in the Great Powers; they never believed in a European procurement of justice, liberty and peace: they *did* look to America for all this —and for infinitely more. It was the pathetic belief of the peoples international that we were they who would redeem the world. Never had the peoples all turned to one people as they turned to us: nor hath it entered into the heart of America how universal and how radical, how tragic and uncreative, is the disappointment we have wrought in all the earth by our apostacy to the Promise.

IV

Yet the blame is not primarily ours. The Entente Powers wanted our men; they wanted our money; they did not want our reasons for entering the war. They wanted the prestige of Wilson; they wanted the loan of Wilson's power—the material usufruct of his current moral sovereignty over the world: they did not want Wilson, they did not want his principles. They had no thought regarding either Wilson or ourselves except that

of exploiting our idealisms for their own imperial pre-
dations. And there is no use further blinking the brutal
truth of the matter—the truth that, as regards both the
war and the execution of the peace, the predominant
purpose of the Entente Powers was to lay upon us as
much as possible of the human and the monetary cost of
their varied schemes of military and capitalist expansion.

Nor did the Powers ever estimate us highly in secret.
The governments and the governors never believed in
either our diplomatic capacity or our understanding of
the world. Clemenceau's opinion of the Germans was
not a whit more derisive than his candid opinion of us.
Lloyd George believed us to be fools, and acted upon his
belief; and for this belief we surely gave him good
grounds. We had just one sincere friend in Europe—
Italy; and we were tricked into estranging that friend
by the intrigues of Italy's allies.

V

Yet the peoples of Europe and Asia do not believe
America deliberately apostate. They know we were
duped, our idealisms detestably exploited. They believe
that Wilson was deceived and defeated, as they themselves were deceived and defeated. They believe that we
of America have not so much turned back upon our opportunity as that we are passing through a provisional
reaction against the diplomatic and monetary policies of
Europe. Marvellous as it may seem, notwithstanding the
catastrophe of Paris, the hope in us still endures: the
faith in America persists. These ravaged peoples, even
amidst the tortures and terrors devouring them, still
expect that we are they who will redeem the world.
They still trust that the promise wherewith we entered
the war will be by us fulfilled. They still look for us to
stretch forth our hands for their healing. Deeper than
the disgust with Paris, deeper than the bitter reaction
which the defeat of Wilson and our withdrawal have
produced, this bruised but still vital hope in America
throbs in the world's heart.

Indeed, we may say that the Wilson Peace was actu-

ally made in the minds of the peoples, even while it was
exteriorly unmade by the governments. It is still there
in the world's mind—the Wilson Peace—and there it will
creatively continue. That which Wilson has done cannot finally be undone. That which came out of America
can never be recalled. Even if our help be withdrawn,
the fatality will be ours, the ultimate effectuation of
the peace promise by Wilson is as certain as the continued
existence of humanity.

VI

So the burden and the responsibility of America remain; and from that burden and that responsibility
there is no righteous escape. For the vows of consecration which we make, whether as individuals or as
societies or as nations, we can never disavow. Either
willingly or retributively, we must fulfil them; we must
pay the uttermost farthing of our pledge. Our vows
become the very laws of our being: they follow us unto
their fulfilment or our destruction.

The sins of others cannot excuse us. The worst that
the diplomacy of Europe has done, or may yet do, in no
wise cancels our redemptive obligation. Nor are they
cancelled by the conduct of Wilson: let Wilson's methods
be as autocratic and un-American as his opponents proclaim them to be; let him be as ruthless toward his real
friends as you please; he no less laid upon us a burden
that is divine, and a burden that we accepted by our participation in the war and the Conference. We have
placed our offerings on humanity's eternal altar: they
cannot now be taken back: they belong to God's fruitful fires.

We came promising the freedom of international
faith to Europe, and the resultant age of good-will: we
have left Europe in the ancient bonds—in the ancient
bonds made bitter and fast—and in manifold misery and
death. And into all this hell we shall ourselves descend,
inevitably and deservedly, if we do not return to Europe's
rescue and redemption. If we hold apart, we shall need
a place of repentance profounder than that needed or

besought by Germany. For upon us shone a light that on Germany had not dawned; and it is against the light that we have sinned by our withdrawal, while it was in the darkness that Germany committed her great transgression.

Whether we will or no, without regard to our hates and resentments or desires, there is now open to America but two destinies: one is our suicide as a nation—a suicide both spiritual and economic; the other is the fulfilment of our pledge to the world—our pledge to achieve a world without war, a world consisting wholly of one family of free nations, a world prepared for the approach of the order implicit in the universal presence of the Christ. If we accept our burden, we shall be infinitely enhanced by it; if we reject our burden we shall be crushed by it, mayhap beyond early redemption.

VII

We have already incurred a heavy guilt by our participation in the long after-war blockade of the peoples east of the Rhine. It was sin enough to have consented to the construction of a treaty writ, at best, according to the law of an eye for an eye and a tooth for a tooth; for we could have forced a peace which, while pronouncing just judgment upon the Central Powers, while exacting reparations for the ruin they had wrought, would at the same time have tempered those judgments and reparations with redemptive execution—with an administration tending to spiritual and physical regeneration. But our failure went immeasureably beyond this. We consented that populations reaching from the Rhine to the Volga, and from the Arctic seas to the Adriatic, should be reduced to material and moral despair; should die in festering famine and every kind of misery—and this in order that one Entente Power might wreak revenge and gain a Shylock's indemnity, and another Entente Power seize the economic hegemony of two continents. The blood of Europe's mothers and children, of helpless millions of them, cries out against our apostacy. We are responsible for this European and Asiatic perdition: we could have prevented the perdition and did not.

VIII

The insistent reiteration of these chapters is, that the world is now so bound up together that no nation can suffer oppresion or disorganization without all nations suffering the same. We are members one of another, whether we will or no. No people is safe until all peoples are safe. The strong peoples must bear the burdens of the weak, or else themselves become, at last, weaker than the weak.

America is the strong nation of the world. We had —and in so far as we have lost may regain—the world's confidence. Our Chieftain pledged us to the world's service—pledged us with an authority higher than his own, and to-day resurgent in the world's increasing crisis. We have thousands of eager and disinterested young men,—industrial administrators and engineers,—civil and commercial servants and educators,—who would rejoice to go redemptively to the tribes and peoples now calling to us, even from the earth's rims and edges. At no time in history has a nation been so equipped, and therefore so responsible, for world-service as is the American nation at the present moment.

And from our midst has gone forth an immortal example. The Crusades of the Middle Ages pale into a mere romanticism when compared with the crusade of Mr. Hoover and his Commission against the starvation and the anarchy of a continent. Mr. Hoover and his co-workers have honored America infinitely more than America has honored them. And why should we not, as a nation, use the great spiritual asset afforded by their example? Why not set before our youth, before our educational and industrial institutions, the purpose, the prospect, the truly divine mission, of the political and economic redemption and co-ordination of the peoples walking impoverished and oppressed amidst death and deep darkness? The enshrinement of such an example, the acceptance of such a mission, would make for every kind of enlargement and ennoblement through our whole national life. And it would make for peace, for ultimate and permanent disarmament, as would nothing else proposed to or by the nations.

Even concessions granted to financial groups, under such administration as we would thus undertake, would in some degree make for the healing of the peoples. Even if their mines, railways and industries be developed with a view to our profit, the development would carry with it an education in organization and responsibility, in mutual forbearance and understanding, that might outweigh the evils of capitalist initiative and control. Moreover, such co-operation of financial investment and spiritual adventure, on the part of a great nation, would contribute towards the evolution of new national and international forms.

IX

At the time of Prinkipo, there was apprehension on the part of some of us lest peace with Soviet Russia should be brought about in connection with great concessions to a certain financial group. Yet now looking back upon what has since taken place—looking upon the red to-day of Russia and into the redder to-morrow, —I am not sure but that the arrangement, questionable as it was, would have been wisest provisional solution of our relation to the Russian problem. If the mission of Mr. Bullitt has been frankly announced and openly undertaken; if the proposition of the Soviet Government had been candidly stated before and by the Conference; if the phenomenally competent Lenin and his colleagues had been permitted to co-operate with an industrial administration of Russia by American experts and financiers; we might have seen coming forth, born of this co-operation of Communist Russia with American capital, a new and uniting industrial development. I, as one of the most antagonistic at the time this possibility was debated, could now wish that we might witness the mutually modifying effects of the candid co-working of American capital with the Russian Communist State. In any case, how infinitely less wasteful and more honorable such an experiment would have been than our subsequent participation in the foreign invasions and civil wars of tortured Russia, and in a blockade which may result in the starvation of much of the child-population of that fallen Empire.

X

Howbeit, whether or no an American capitalist experiment would have been well for Russia, certainly the worst that could have been done, either for Russia or for ourselves, that we have done. And we have done this with an ignorance and under a terror that are without excuse. The best minds of Europe, even of the most conservative cast, have demanded an opposite course of their governments. Mr. Asquith, in his speeches to the electorate which returned him to Parliament by an overwhelming majority, explicity advocated a complete peace and the resumption of normal relations with Russia by the British Government. Admiral Lord Fisher had previously declared bolshevism to be merely the reaction from repressed freedom, and that the cure for bolshevism was intercourse with the world. One of the first pronouncements of Premier Giolitti, on coming back into power in Italy, was to the effect that Italy should enter immediately upon normal diplomatic and commercial relations with Russia. President Mazaryk—than whom no nobler or wiser European spokesman lives to-day—has again and again pronounced against our subsidized civil wars in Russia; and he has repeatedly besought the deliverance of the Russian peoples from every exterior menace, in order that they might work out their political and economic salvation. Notwithstanding the fact that Attorney-General Palmer would be obliged—according to his record—instantly to hale Mr. Asquith, Admiral Fisher, Premier Giolitti and President Mazaryk to prison, and that without trial, should they have the temerity to set foot on our shores, I nevertheless insist that the mind of these men regarding Russia is worthy of American attention.

XI

But we are apostate not only in this—that we had opportunity to demand that the question of Russia's future be left to Russians themselves; and that in failing so to act, we were false to our own Revolution, and also to the principles which Wilson had announced. A greater dishonesty was ours: while crying against foreign entanglements, we were at the same time a participant in the worst, the most degrading entanglement of our history or of the war. There is nothing more evilly entangling, indeed, than the actions of the Entente and of America towards Russia. The Entente has secretly traded with Soviet Russia with the one hand, and with the other secretly supplied the enemies of this same Russia with American means and instruments of war. We and they starved the Russian peoples by our blockades and presented the starvation as the result of Soviet administration. Even assuming as true the tales of the bolshevist terror, we, America and France and England, by the methods we have pursued against Soviet Russia, have literally slain our millions, and slain them infamously, where the bolshevists have slain their tens. And America had no more right, in national morals or in international law, to furnish soldiers and munitions to kill Russian peasants than had Soviet Russia to send an army to deliver America from the legal anarchy and terror created by her own Department of Justice.

<h2 style="text-align:center">XII</h2>

Again, our recent unconsidered rejection of responsibility for Armenia will not ultimately be regarded as other than an apostacy. We had given the world to understand that we were fighting for the deliverance of oppressed peoples from alien or foreign domination. The Armenians had peculiarly suffered, and suffered long, from the rule by massacre which both the Turk and Czarist Russia had practised. We had also encouraged the Armenians to expect our protection. To have accepted the mandate was the least that we could have done. We have rejected indeed, on the ostensible ground of disinteresting ourselves in the Asiatic contentions and intrigues of the it, with little or no discussion, with scarcely a thought sources and mineral riches of Western Asia is beyond dispute. Nothing can be said to mitigate the mercilessness, the meanness, the total wickedness of these on-going struggles. Whole tribes and peoples, vast regions already become but little more than the graveyards of nations, are now the subject of diplomatic wars no less red in their results than Prussian invasions and Turkish massacres. The present diplomatic war between France and England over Asiatic concessions may prove more atrocious in the end, more fatal by far to civilization, than the battles of the Marne and the Somme. It is not to be wondered at, therefore, that we shrank from being involved.

Yet our qualified sovereignity in Armenia is the one thing that might have called a halt to the evil strife. The mere presence of an American executive and of the American flag might have changed the whole course of both Asiatic and European procedure. I believe the new tide of Turkish massacre would have turned back at our bidding, even if we had not had a regiment in Asia Minor. And we could have demanded, in accepting the mandate, an integral and undivided Armenia, including Cilicia and Russian Armenia: and neither Britain nor France would have dared say us nay.

Our rejection of the Armenian mandate was ignoble— even though we were proffered an Armenian remnant shorn of economic value; even though we should have been saddled with an unprofitably military and financial responsibility. Had we accepted what was truly our responsibility, had we undertaken the fulfilment of our high calling, we should have made even the Armenian remnant our foothold for the deliverance of many peoples. We could have saved not only Armenia; we could have rescued Western Asia from massacre and anarchy. We would also there have stood in a place of incontestable moral authority over both continents.

XIII

Nor is it only our rejection of the Armenian mandate that rises up against us in judgment. Sooner or later, it will be a source of common and profound regret that the whole question of American mandates was not more fully presented and widely understood. It is against a great current of traditional feeling that President Wilson has had to stand, in raising this question at all. But he did well to raise it: in this, as in other things, he was wiser than his day and generation. For America cannot, except at her own peril, refuse to undertake the administration of weaker and less developed peoples, no matter how far they be from our shores—especially as these peoples are appealing for our administration as their sole hope for the future; as their only refuge from worse oppressions, further massacres, and final extinction.

XIV

We are not without precedent. What we have done in Cuba and the Philippines can be set down as high examples of the protection and development of weak peoples by a strong people. Though I was among the college men who thought our war with Spain needless and reprehensible, though I opposed the Philippines occupation, I can only be truthful by now praising things we have done for the Cubans and Philippinos.

With the invocative precedent of the Philippines before us, we should enter, and with confidence and hope, upon the government of such peoples as the Armenians, the Albanians, the Macedonians—even unto the administrative occupation of Constantinople, the liquidation of the Turkish Empire, and the organization and redemption of all the peoples formerly under Turkish rule. And, in one sense, we should be proceeding without precedent. We should not be establishing the old order of protectorates created by conquest: we should be giving to peoples asking for our occupation—asking with all the piteous energy that remains to them after centuries of administrative tyranny, massacre, and anarchy. Nor would our accepting mandates make only for their political and economic salvation: it would infinitely enhance, to each of us as citizens, the value of our own national life.

XV

The burden of becoming an international missionary, the saviour and restorer of long oppressed and dismembered peoples, is surely laid upon us. In the minds of all peoples, we are nationally pledged to this mission. It was implied by the purpose and the principles whereby we entered the war. The shattered and starving nationalities believe this to be the logic of all we fought for. We are divinely bound to be faithful to their faith. If now we look only to the saving of our own national life, we shall lose it. If we freely lose our national life in the service of other national lives, we shall find it, and find it gloriously.

This burden is not lessened but enhanced by our failure to effectuate our program at Paris. That failure, it is true, as history will one day record, was not wholly our fault. We went to Paris sincerely bent upon the creation of a new world. Our failure to fulfil the purpose for which we went to the Peace Table is due to the irreconcilable difference between the historic psychology of European governments and the common mind of America. Between the American conception of international relations and European diplomacy is fixed a gulf too great to be bridged. But though the recoil of the American mind from this diplomacy is understandable, it would be woeful to the world, and ultimately worse for ourselves, if the consequence should be our refusal of our international burden. Then, indeed, would we have gone to Paris in vain, and our armies would have fought in vain.

IX
THE ANGLO-SAXON BROTHERHOOD

The most vital question for the English-speaking peoples to-day is that of Anglo-American unity. Beside this question all others are mere side issues. What the other nations will do will depend on the political, social, and commercial attitude of Great Britain and the United States.

Francis Grierson.

I have tried to give some exposition of what seems to me the greatest problem of the age as it is presented in Europe, the problem of the relationship of capital and labor. I believe the stability of the present order of society, the maintenance of a society based upon the principle of property rights, is bound up with the way this problem is worked out in Europe. We cannot stand a world apart in its solution. Indeed, we cannot stand a world apart in any sense. No matter how self-sufficient we may believe ourselves to be, no matter how unlimited are the resources of natural wealth within us, we are inevitably part of what is coming to be a very small world, a world in which ideas travel with a freedom and rapidity that must force us to become internationalists in our views, and must govern us by international considerations, whatever may be our natural tendencies to Chauvinism or our disposition toward an insular isolation and security.

Frank A. Vanderlip.

There are few reflections which so chasten the modern mind or so well illuminate the slow continuity of the human race as the recognition of the fact that a thousand years ago Alfred had fixed political conceptions and ideals, to grasp which is still essential for the redress of modern wrongs.

Warwick H. Draper.

IX

THE ANGLO-SAXON BROTHERHOOD

I.

Some months before the armistice, the German Kaiser proclaimed the essential war to be between the German and the Anglo-Saxon ideals. It would decide, he was convinced, whether the world was to become German or Anglo-Saxon.

The Kaiser spoke truly. The war was indeed between the German and the Anglo-Saxon ideals,—both of life and of government; and, in a higher sense than either the German or the Englishman knew, for world-hegemony. And this is true notwithstanding our historic hypocrisy regarding our ideals, or a possible new idealization of the German mind and motivity.

The German ideal was that of an autocratic state, resolving itself into a perfectable and finally perfect mechanism, benevolent in its operations and opulent in its results, yet reducing the individual to a spiritual and intellectual conscript, to an industrial and military automaton. It indeed aimed at an efficiency so compulsive and inclusive, so materially providential also, that it would relieve the individual of both necessity and occasion for thought.

The Anglo-Saxon's ideal was the antithesis of the German's. Reaching back to the times between Venerable Bede and Alfred the Great, and afterwards highly expounded by John Milton and then by John Stuart Mill, it really rooted itself in those principles and associations expressed in the Sermon on the Mount. King Alfred professedly received from Christ his whole conception of society and government, and indeed of the whole relational life of man.

II

It was in defence of this ideal the Anglo-Saxon peoples were called to arms. The war opened the gates of Anglo-Saxon opportunity and presented the climax of Anglo-Saxon responsibility. It behoved the English race to undertake a world wholly ordered and wholly brothered, yet a world infinitely dividious and varied in its individual, national and social types. To fall back upon the mind of King Alfred, the war summoned the Anglo-Saxon peoples to a unity between themselves, and thence to an apostolate, to a new historical process, whereby the world would at last be rendered up to God as the express image and glory of his Christ.

And against this Anglo-Saxon possibility, both the war and the diplomatic struggle of Germany were directed. In her pourparlers with private spokesmen of her enemies, in her efforts for a premature peace, her first hope was that of bringing the interior questions of the British Empire to the Conference Table. She schemed to place the problems of Ireland and Egypt and India upon the same basis as the problems of Alsace-Lorraine and Poland, Belgium and Serbia, Albania and Armenia. She counted upon the conference as a *pou sto* for the accomplishment of British imperial disruption.

But her intention did not stop there. Each peace manœuvre was a search for some vantage ground wherefrom to strike division between the two great branches of the Anglo-Saxon family. She conceived of the conference as first of all a place for the psychological mobilization of the nations against the British Empire; but, secondly and more fundamentally, she sought the breaking of the ties that bind—or that then bound—America and Britain together.

In the pursuance of her first purpose, her effort was to force England into a position that would compel her to apologize for her Empire and yield up her world-politic. If Germany could have accomplished this, if she could have forced the British Empire into a position of apology, then the primary German diplomatic quest would have been fulfilled. And if, along with this, Germany could have shattered the confidence and hope of unity between the two great members of the Anglo-Saxon race, she would have considered the foundations of her own world-dominion as thus surely laid.

III

It will be noticed that I have used the subjunctive. But the use is largely formal. For the German succeeded. Or, rather, what the German could not accomplish against England has been by England accomplished against herself. In any case, whether it be a German achievement or the result of Anglo-Saxon apostacy, certain it is that these two German desires have been fulfilled:—England has been called to account for her Empire; she stands judged before all peoples for her imperialistic seizures since the peace of Versailles was signed; and the two great branches of the Anglo-Saxon family are, at least according to the American mind, now sharply divided against each other.

American hostility to Great Britain is more intense and bitter than at any time since the Revolution. And there is an element in our American national life that is consciously preparing to contest with Great Britain the financial hegemony of the planet. All the old contentions between England and America are recalled; all the sins of England against America are rehearsed; and the fact that we owe to Great Britain much of our immunity from attack, and that even the enforcement of the Munroe Doctrine is largely due to Great Britain—all this is either unknown or forgoten.

IV

Nor does the rehearsal stop with the Peace of Versailles. It is perceived that the world-war itself results from England's diplomatic past. It is England that put back Europe a hundred years, if not a half-millenium, by the overthrow of Napoleon—the most enlightened and liberal of Europe's civil rulers after the greater Romans, and the one man of power who foresaw the future of the peoples. It is England that saved and supported the Prussia which Napoleon believed to be the next great enemy of civilization—regretting that he had not extinguished the Prussian State and its dynasty when he had the power so to do. It is England that kept silent at the critical moment of 1870, and allowed Prussia to tear Alsace-Lorraine from the side of France. Indeed, the war in which Great Britain has for five years been engaged, at the sacrifice of so vast number of English lives and so much of English treasure, was fought against the Prussia which British policy had partly built up. The same British policy had always preserved the Austro-Hungarian Monarchy against all comers, and had prevented the Balkan peoples from achieving freedom and federation. And England kept the Turk in Europe—the Turk to whom, even now, we must probably surrender Western Asia, or else engage in new wars.

V

It must be discerned and admitted, too, that there is a profound if unconscious spiritual element in our present anti-British state of mind. It is more than the Briton's manifest sense of superiority we resent: it is more than his diplomatic iniquities: it is a resentment of hypocrisy less recognized and more intimate. It has to do with ancient moral assumptions—with traditions of British fair-play and honor. In the validity of these traditions we no longer believe as we did. The notion of the Briton that he "plays the game," and that other peoples do not, has become to the American obnoxious. For the American now feels that this is the one thing which the usual Briton never does, either as an imperial representative or as a private person; we do not behold him playing the straight game in his political dealings with other nations or their citizens; he is seen covertly to be using them for English ends. I am not discussing the right or wrong of this American feeling: I am only stating it—stating that confidence in British political honesty or commercial frankness has been uprooted from the average American's mind. He has discovered, he thinks, the predatory persistence, the insinuating national covetousness, which the Briton has more or less concealed in centuries of self-complacent civility.

And certain it is, that whatever the American proves to be—once the real American comes into being—he will be other than merely Anglo-Saxon. The American, when he comes to his intellectual and spiritual selfhood, will be infinitely more candid than was ever the Englishman. America is struggling, however perversely and blindly, for a candor, at once spiritual and national, that hitherto has never obtained between nations.

VI

Yet, when all this has been said, when the whole condemnation has been made, when the Englishman has been well brought to judgment, certain counter-things are emphatically to be considered. The first is, that the Englishman is tempermentally more liberal by far than the American: he has acquired a toleration for other sorts of humanity, for every kind of opinion, for everything that mortals choose to think or say, that is quite alien to American mentality or experience. A second thing to be kept in mind is that war between Great Britain and America, should such a conclusive calamity befall the world, might well result in the practical extinction of humanity. A third thing to be pondered,—to be unreservedly admitted,—is the fact that our present rampant remembrance of Britain's aggresions and sins springs from no Altrurian design: it is rehearsed by our journals and politicians to cover a developing vaster imperialism of our own.

VII

Let us not overlook, in this critical moment, the Englishman's indisputable genius for colonial administration. In this, as in his capacity for political and institutional evolution, he has no equal. No other people has proved as capable as the English of some understanding of alien peoples, and of procuring somewhat of their well-being. After all the just criticisms have been made; after all the sad blunders have been tabulated and verified; after the concessionnaires and moneylenders have had their due condemnation; it nevertheless remains true that, when compared with other imperialisms, both ancient and modern, the balance is on the credit side of British administration. As an instance, the course of England in South Africa,—giving entire self-government to the Boers she had conquered,—will remain a marvel of fine and foreseeing statesmanship.

True, it is time that Egypt be made independent or autonomous; and time that India and Ireland be placed among the self-governing British dominions. But, having said this, it must also be said that the peoples of Egypt and India have had more of justice and security, more of moral and material well-being, under British rule than they have had during most of the centuries of other government or administration—whether native or foreign. The British Empire, with all its lack of definition and direction, with all the English sloth in the adaptation of the ideal, is no less a rude microcosm of the world-community for which the Spirit of History strives.

VIII

It is time that we of the great Republic, springing as we do from the English bosom, should join the Mother-Commonwealth in a new and unifying world-policy. But we must perceive that,—if Anglo-Saxon unity is to be,—its realization is our American responsibility. The responsibility is England's, of course, but the present circumstances of the world have made it initiatively ours. And when I speak of Anglo-Saxon unity, I hardly need qualify the term. I mean, naturally, the fellowship of those commonwealths which, however composite their populations, are of distinctly English origin and foundation and speak the English tongue.

It is by this union of Anglo-Saxon peoples, and by this only, that the divine end against which Germany strove can be in the near generations achieved and thus world-community of free and co-operative nations rise from dream to reality. And the Anglo-Saxon brotherhood, should it soon be realized, might even yet save the world from the war's worst woes, and from the deeper woes of a peace worse than the war. Once we have purified ourselves by the flame through which we have passed, and mayhap the fiercer flames to come, then the healing and the harmonization of the world becomes our instant and inclusive vocation. And against this vocation,—calling as it will for a collective consecration unknown to human annals,—neither our present contrarieties nor ancient contradictions will be able to stand.

In the pursuit of the war, we have gathered up into our commonwealths, girding the globe as they do, the knowledge and the urgence of all the better forces of history—the forces making for a new and higher place of world-evolution. It is ours to make these forces our common *élan vital,* and to make the total well-being of mankind, including the German and excluding none, our common reason for being. It is given unto us, if we will receive it, to project to-day the new historical process—a process which, ere its course be run, shall raise man from creatureship to creatorship, and convert our whole planetary life into God's well-fulfilled vision.

X.
THE FINAL HOPE.

And all ways of the world are false and blind
And barred and bounded to a mean ambition,
Which knows no more magnificent prize than mere
Exclusive profits and prosperities;
And all ways of the soul are ways of truth,
Which whoso treads them out shall learn to know
What excellence there is within himself
Which finds no hope or having tolerable
That all men may not share on equal terms!

George Cabot Lodge in "Herakles."

And now, Lord, look upon their threatenings: and grant unto thy servants to speak thy word with all boldness, while thou stretchest forth thy hand to heal; and that signs and wonders may be done through the name of thy holy Servant Jesus. And when they had prayed, the place was shaken wherein they were gathered together; and they were all filled with the Holy Ghost, and they spake the word of God with boldness.

And the multitude of them that believed were of one heart and soul: and not one of them said that aught of the things which he possessed was his own; but they had all things common. And with great power gave the apostles their witness of the resurrection of the Lord Jesus: and great grace was upon them all. For neither was there among them any that lacked: for as many as were possessors of lands or houses sold them, and brought the prices of the things that were sold, and laid them at the apostles' feet: and distribution was made unto each, according as any one had need.

The Acts of the Apostles.

X

THE FINAL HOPE

I

IN long ago vagabond days, wherein I pitched my tent with the Syrian and the Arab, I returned to America with a cane carved from an ancient olive tree not far from Jerusalem. Always, wherever I lived, the cane stood unused in a corner of my study. But when I started from Geneva to Paris, in the early days of the Conference, it was with my memorial stick in hand. "Why are you taking that particular cane?" demanded my son of sixteen years. "I am going to Paris to set up the kingdom of heaven," was my whimsical yet heartful reply,"and this staff from the country of Jesus is a symbol of my purpose." "See that they don't break it, father," retorted the less credulous boy. "They" did break it. Arriving at the Crillon, and attempting to enter with my portfolio in one hand and my cane in the other, I collided first with one of the Commission's military attachês and then, if I remember rightly, with one of its "economic advisers." They were awesome beings, both of them, bursting with importance: and, pushing angrily by, they wheeled the door violently upon my Jerusalem cane: it fell in fragments at my feet. Curiously and instantly, fell also my faith, as unsupporting as my shattered stick—a faith so incredibly naive, retrospectively looked at, as to make me doubtful if ever I should have been allowed to leave my mother's knee.

For the kingdom of heaven was far from the men who contorted the travesty of Versailles. Nor it is strange, in the light of the secret motives and processes of the Conference, that universal division and discord, not unity and concord, is their gift to the world. For it was the material mind, the material motive, that predicated the Conference proceedings, and that produced and inscribed its conclusions. And in the material mind and motive, in the individual and national egotisms issuing therefrom, there is no uniting principle. The material motive always divides: it is the spiritual motive only that unites. It is the material motive that shapes the swords of division—that creates the mine and the thine of individuals and classes and nations. And from mine and thine come the wars, and the most of mortal woes; and from mine and thine comes also the advancing dissolution of the present world—the social disintegration precipitated by the war and sealed by the Great Powers at Paris.

II

Yet Paris, after all, was but a reflex of our total civilization. The Conference and its works are but a disclosure of that disablement of the soul which history will finally ascribe to our civilization as its final achievement and the cause of its dissolution. Or, to put it differently, we may say that our civilization has modernly evolved without reference to the soul: it has taken no account of our essential humanhood. Or, rather, our industrial and social machinery has reduced the souls of men to servitude, and of the souls of nations made grist for the money-lender's mill. Progress, for some generations, has been synonymous with the soul's descent into economic slavery and social cowardice. And it is because of this, and for the release and remanning of the soul, and as a fearful prelude to the world-soul's birth, that our civilization is given over to a destruction that must ultimately prove divinely creative.

For what is happening to the essential man is all that matters. Historic institutions and policies have all been judged, in the end, by what account they could give of him—but what account they could give of the soul—by what account the soul could give of itself in the midst of them. The world's catastrophe is but a calling of the world's managers—its owners, its diplomats, its governments—to that judgment-seat unto which the soul is the only concern. And the general dissolution is the consequence of their having no answer to give to the Judge thereon seated.

It is but for the making of man, indeed, that our

universe exists; and civilization is dissolving through
its collision with that universal reason for being. And
the collisional action will continue until, from highest
pinnacle to deepest foundation, our present world-order
becomes but a dusty memory. Nor will another and new
order be any the more able to stand, no matter how
radically it differs from the old, unless the motive of
its laws and machines be the enabling invocation of the
soul. Nothing the peoples or leaders may henceforth
make will be able to justify or establish its existence,
except so far as it makes for the soul's release and
expansion; for the soul's march from freedom to freedom; for the achievement of that manhood which, pat-
terned once and for ever in Palestine, and looming now
anew and larger over the world, is our one eternal standard of measure.

III

But you will ask, since we know the great betrayal,
and since the general chaos we know, and the thicker
financial yoke also, what hope have we—with what promise can we path anew our mortal pilgrimage? What
has humanity gotten out of the great catastrophe, after
all, that may inspire any solacing or renewing effort?
We have this: the preparing definite end of a world
in which any kind of bondage can be. It is true we are
in the wilderness still. But it is also true that we are
out of Egypt: we are on our way to the undisclosed
promised land. Whether our years in the wilderness be
few or many depends, of course, upon ourselves—upon
what quality and collectivity of will the peoples develop.
Nevertheless, it is for the soul to rejoice and not lament
the dissolution of the present order. For our civilization
cannot be reformed: it can only be dissolved, or else
undergo an entire inner and outer regeneration. It has
deceived and dazzled by the height and the might of its
material achievements; but it is no less corrupt and
false in its fundamental motivities as well as in its
methods and institutions. Its material-mindedness is
fatal not only to the spiritual existence of humanity:
it is false to even a true material continuity.

IV

Yes, the old creeds, the old laws, the old ways of directing the affairs of men, they are all dying or dead: let them pass, let the dead bury them. The sword they shaped has failed, the diplomat has failed, the financier has failed, the intellectual and the expert have failed also: leave them to their failures. Not by clinging to the world that is crumbling can you save what spiritual treasure the past has preserved, or what good the present holds, or work these into the new and nobler world-structure. *It is not the salvation of the old but the creation of the new to which we are now called. It is neither reformation nor spiritual recovery that awaits us: it is the utter new birth of mankind.*

V

So upon the failure of Paris we may pivot hopes for the future. The world's present despair carries in itself the portent, the germinative process, of a new quality of collective reflection, purpose and action. The vanity and vampirism of the old order, its loathesomeness and ugliness, the fraudulency and meanness of the methods by which it has maintained itself, these to-day stand forth nakedly. By our abandonment of hope for this vile order, we reach forward, even if but blindly, even if but blunderingly, to an order wherein the abundant life may be commonly lived.

Indeed, the law of the new earth is already upon us. We may deny the new law; we may delay the new earth. But the law cannot be revoked or evaded. Nor can the old earth be restored. We may accept the new world and live; we may disavow it and die; but there is no escape from its summons. And there is no turning back: there is only a going forward. Fearfully we may go and perforcedly, or manfully and burningly; but howsoever we go, with what lack or strength of heart, it is only the onward way lies open—that, or the descent of the world into a death from which there is no near resurrection.

VI

But the waiting new world cannot come through division—through our reaching again for the sword. Let us remember that it was under the spell of the sword, while our attention was highly fixed upon freedoms not yet achieved, and amid unprecedented military heroisms and civil martyrdoms, that the usurers made strong the new fetters they now fasten upon the nations. If we take again the sword, it is the usurers we shall again serve, and ourselves and not they shall be defeated.

The work of the sword, such as it is, is done. If it be true that only war can overthrow the old and the evil,—because men do not willingly go forth from the forms that are outworn and corrupt,—that is all that war can do. The sword can only destroy, it cannot create. It hath no power to construct or establish the good or the enduring.

The forms of the new world will not be fashioned by the force of armies. Brotherhood cannot issue from war betwen states, from war between classes. Not through division but through union, not through conflict but through conciliation and co-operation, not through more death but through more life, not down the broad ways of hate but up the highways of love, and by climbing them hardly, shall we envision the new heaven and effectuate the new earth.

VII

Nor can the new world be brought forth by the ongoing struggles of either the new or the changed nationalities. It is not for an actual freedom these now fight; not for true self-determination, true self-expression: it is for coal and iron and oil, for potash and cotton, for copper and gold: for the yet remaining undeveloped advantages and material dominance. These racial strifes, these relentless national egotisms, adding destruction to destruction as they do, are but the offensive and defensive cupidities which the Great Powers, each for its own vile but veiled ends, have artificially instilled among the lesser peoples.

By these Powers, or by the assembled Appetites they served at Paris, the whole spirit and meaning of nationality has been perverted. Each nationality came clamourously to Paris with its catalogue of rights—the rights consisting, in the mind of each, of all and whatsoever it could seize and hold. No European people came seeking, first of all, the fulfilment of the ripe desire for a universal republic of good-will; for the union of all peoples in a mutuality and equality of opportunity and progress. Not one nationality came with a gesture of renunciation—came willing to make concessions for the sake of achieving a well-being international; for the sake of finding a freedom, of devising a wealth, of procuring a health, that should accrue to all peoples, making them co-workers and friends one with another. Not one came eager for the rights of others as well as for the rights it claimed for itself.

Even when it came to principles, each European power, great and small, looked upon the Fourteen Points as something to use in obtaining for itself the largest possible territorial, material and military expansion. Each had in view the selfish gain that could be wrested from a particularist application of the Points. Each laid upon Wilson the burden of its claims and the responsibility for realizing them. Each demanded his help in getting the thing it wanted for itself. Not one offered to help him get the thing he so tremendously wanted for the world, and which was so indispensable to the world's rational ongoing.

Whence the nations, great and small alike, are losing their lives through falsely saving them—through the concentration of each upon its own material advantage, its own territorial enlargement. The nation that would now renounce itself for the common healing of all; the nation that would now base itself upon an honest application of the Fourteen Points; the nation that would now undertake the actual realization of Christ's law of love in international relations;—that nation, however small, whatever its past, would have the spiritual leadership of Europe, if not of the world. Such a gesture of renunciation, divine in its quality and consequence, irresistible and regenerative in the power of its appeal, would magically liberate the common impulse of goodwill now supressed, and only needing release in order to function itself quickly and manifoldly, and to constitute the world anew and divinely. Such a gesture, quickening the nations to a health and a wealth both spiritual and physical, would indeed predicate, mayhap precipitate, the approach of a literal kingdom of heaven upon earth; whence the universal hate and hatefulness which Paris engendered would vanish, and the love that was in Christ, the love that is Christ, newly risen and incarnate in the whole human collectivity, would go forth unto its eternal increase.

VIII

It is upon the youth of Europe that the burden of the uniting renunciations must fall, and by whom the divine initiative must be taken. It is by the young men and women of these nations, reaching hands across every kind of frontier, psychical and social as well as geographical and political, that the capitalized hate must be overthrown. It is these who must give office, give function and power, to the yet unorganized good-will, the latent social love, immanent and omnipresent in the peoples. It is these who must wield the wands before which the uncreative forces and the accumulating terrors of this retributive time shall flee away. It is these who must interpret the world's awakening communist mind, and follow and transmute and transfigure it; for this mind, though its early ways be rude and red and ruinous, is yet predestined to universal conquest, and is charged with the elements of the world's Christly renewal.

IX

I have said the youth of Europe, and it is to these I now make appeal. But let me say, at this point, that not for a moment do I think that the American crusade for a free and clean world is abandoned. The crusade is turned back upon itself, for a time, beaten and put to shame. It was beaten, I say, for the youth of America did not willingly fail their ideal. They were cheated and exploited by the same forces whereby the youth of Europe and the hope of the world were cheated and exploited. But not for always, not for long: this American youth will rise again, and rise anointed and resolute—will rise with a knowledge of who its real foes are, and of the worlded thing it has yet to do.

I know I am safe in pledging this—in pledging the fellowship of Young America to Young Europe for the vastly diviner issues than those apparent or vocal in the war. I stand in no doubt of America—of ultimate America. I am as strong in my belief now as I was in 1917, "that the iron of God has gone deep into the American soul," and that in the strength thereof we shall again go forth to "close up the old world and its political methods and to lay living foundations for a world of democratic and co-operative peoples." I am as certain now as I was then that our American youth were "moved by a sense of responsibility new and strange in the conscience and conduct of nations." That sense of responsibility, though dissipated now, will yet return to its former appointments, reintegrate and triumphant, creating thenceforth its own occasion, its own interpretations and leaderships.

X

Yet, as I have said, it is to the youth of Europe rather than to the youth of America, to whom the urgent new gates of opportunity first open. For the moment, reaction reigns in America, and we are vainly trying to rid ourselves of the tremendous world-burden divinely bound upon us. But Europe, midway between awakening and wondering Asia and reactionary if chosen America, is dissolving and flowing in the melting-pot of the future. It is therefore to the youth of these European states that the "word of the Lord" comes immediately. It is for them to take the new initiative, following not the little Bismarcks or the unmalleable Marxians, neither the triumphant imperialists nor the clamorous nationalists,

but Jesus and John Milton, Lammenais and Mazzini—
and Woodrow Wilson's first principles. It is for an international order wherein love shall be both the directing
intelligence of the state and the law of industrial association. This,—or the doom of the white race in Europe,
Asia and Africa draws near.

That doom has already been sounded upon the pla-
teaux of Asia and by the rivers of Africa: and the
failure of the youth of Europe to see and seize their
opportunity might seal the doom irrevocably. If these
youth prove unequal to their hour, if they choose compromise or reaction rather than new initiative and creation, then they and their lands may be lost in the loosed
Asian tide; whence, after many terrible years, after
the whole family of man has dwelt long in the darkness
now descending, the yellow race, or the brown or even
the black, may bring forth a civilization that shall release
the soul and convoke the new heaven and the new earth.

XI

But the leagued youth of the nations must include in
their purpose, in their searching and profound apprehension, far and fundamentally more than the problems
of peace between States. Even these problems, urgent
and charged with peril as they are, rest back upon primary
industrial conclusions. The industry of Europe is pro-
strate—much of it wrecked beyond early repair; and no
revival or reconstruction is possible along the former
lines of either capitalism or laborism. By the exigencies
of the war, not only has the capitalist management of
industry broken down; not only has the incompetence
of the capitalist control of society been demonstrated;
there has been an equal demonstration of the political
incompetence of orthodox socialism—of the socialism
which proposed an international social reconstruction
through class-revolution; and there has been a like
breakdown of former defensive methods of organized
labor. Both labor and capital--indeed all the functions
and organs and offices of both industrial and political
society—have gone into the pit together. Nor is there

any certain issue therefrom save by the discerning and determined good-will of all classes and conditions, co-operate and co-ordinate.

XII

No class solution of the problems of economic production, distribution and control is now possible. The true interest of no class, of no man, can now be dealt with apart from the true interests of all classes and all men. We are all in the human scrape together; we must get out of it together; else we of this generation shall not get out of it at all. The only way of industrial and social escape is by a purpose, by a program, which includes the willing and comprehending co-operation of every class, of every man, from the topmost to the downmost. Our membership one with another is something we cannot further evade or defer, either in theory or practice. Mankind must henceforth act together as one economic body, one spiritual entity, one planetary family and household—else mankind will perish from the earth.

XIII

The war has precipitated the fact of human indivisibility beyond repeal or recall. We can no more antagonize or ignore it than we antagonize or ignore the air we breathe, the ground we walk upon. And this disclosure of the social and economic indivisibility of mankind constitutes the most drastic, the most radical, the most revolutionary happening of history.

Not that the knowledge of this unity has ever been absent from man: it was long ago cried aloud, both by Christ and the prophets of the farther East: but now it is vocal in every loaf of bread we are able to procure, as well as by the discovery that America dare not let Europe die, lest she herself perish also. We have but faintly apprehended the revolution yet; but it is here, life's most determining and judicative fact. The sooner we discern and acknowledge it, the sooner we shall begin to save the whole race of man from still deeper perdition;

and so much the sooner shall we start upon an ascension into undreamed-of power and prosperity—into a power that, just because it is the activity of associative love, and therefore a spiritual power, must inevitably subdue all natural forces and materials to its commands and use.

XIV

Had the war not been, a new social creation, at first both good and evil, might have resulted from the conflict between the proletaire and the proprietor, between those who operate the tools of production and those who own them and reap the profits. Sooner or later, in the course of an exhaustive historical process—and doubtless at immense spiritual cost and through great loss to our essential humanity—the proletaire would have conquered the possessor. Out of this tyranny, a new and more providential society might, at last, have come.

But not by this way can the new society come now. As I have already pointed out, all the functions and offices, all the classes and controls, all the elements and materials, of the existing society are disintegrating together—are being resolved into one fiery social nebula. And only by a great common and compelling impulse in all classes, each undertaking the utmost reconciliation and co-operation with each, can there come forth that human order which, after all, the whole world desires —an order eventuating in one loving family of adequate and equally advantaged men.

XV

I speak thus imperatively, thus presumptuously if you will, because I perceive mankind to be caught, to-day, between two equally fatal reactions—that of an international Tory capitalism on the one side, and that of an international materialist bolshevism on the other. These, alike super-tyrannous, alike destructive of essential socialism or industrial democracy, are also alike full of death for society and the soul. On the triumph of either of these, waits the spiritual end of our present humanity.

But, though between the deathful two we tremble to-day, it is not needful that either be our choice. We may choose the better way I have already indicated—the way which, running through all the creative movements of our Era, leads to the practice of Christ by the whole economy of man.

It is not easy to speak thus, and one who ventures so to speak may well do so with profound fear and trembling. For threatening indeed is the outlook and the way, at this human juncture, of those who go not with Caiaphas and Herod, nor yet with Barabbas and his followers: for these two camps, hateful as they are to each other, will inevitably howl together to-day, as they did yesterday, for the death or disgrace or whoever speaks the word and seeks the way of reconciliation.

Yet no other word, no other way, can assure the world's renewal. It is this solution—absorbing as it will the essence of socialism and the reality of democracy—issuing in universal association in freedom and universal freedom in association—this, or the present problem of our human life's continuance is insoluble. This solution we must propose and the way thereto follow, or the world is for a long time lost. We must head straight for the kingdom of heaven, or we shall descend into deeper hells than the one wherein we all now blindly flounder: there is no choice, except between these two ways, these two goals. There is no basis for any further human progress except the ground that lies—in the soul of each man and in the soul of the world—between Nazareth and Jerusalem.

XVI

If it be, however, that it is the total passing of a civilization we are now witnessing, there is naught for the pessimist, naught for despair, in this closing of an exhausted era. Let us listen to One who, in a world-crisis not so obvious as ours but transcending it, bade his friends stand about him with hearts neither troubled nor afraid. They were to receive from him a peace so profound, so intimately possessive, yet so burning through with a beaconing love for every human sort, so charged and irradiant with redemptive desire toward every earthly affair or condition, that it would constitute a veritable divine phenomenon, investing its recipients with a comparative super-humanity; with such forsight of the future, also, as would enable them to rejoice in the dissolution of things they hitherto had held sacred and thought permanent, knowing these would give place to a world-order ineffably new and at least tentatively near.

So it may now be with us. The mind that was in him of whom I speak—the mind that made him the Christ —and which mind he fain would have shared with his sorrowing disciples—that mind may be urgently and immovably ours. We, too, may walk hopefully and healingly amidst a corruption and chaos that proclaim the end of a world. Our civilization, being what it is nor showing signs of becoming else, has become the enemy of the soul, is wrecking the essential man. It would seem that it had to be gotten out of the way— out of God's way and man's way—even if by the blood and the flames wherein Saint Peter beheld its finality. Its unregenerate ongoing, sheerly parasitic, and procurable only through manifold imposture and violence, would destroy every reason for the soul's earthly continuance.

This precise issue between the soul and the world-order is the only interpretation,—is indeed the very essence,—of the increasing crisis. *It is the rebellion of the soul that is overturning to-day's civilization: it is the uprising of the essential man that is grinding our systems and institutions unto dust.* And it is not for us to lament but to acclaim the grinding—yea, to hear it as a divine music, and to set our songs to it and sing them for the soul's spreading wings. It would have been indeed for our despair if so false and foul a human order could have continued. Its advancing dissolution but attests the embosoming of our life in a providential care, and should make for faith's infinite enhancement.

It is true that the times would seem not to make for faith, but for utter doubt. The world for the moment seems abandoned. If providential care there be, if an embosoming love be about our humanity, these show neither power nor adequacy. It is rather an encircling hate that now orbs our earth, and the darkness by the hate begotten is deepening into insearchable dread. Yet the experience of both individuals and nations reveals that hate hath no continuating principle, no life or living substance. We know that hate is of the stuff of death, and that unto death its ends all proceed. We perceive, also, as we ponder well the human pilgrimage, that only in love life moves and is—that love and life are in truth the same. We discern, too, that it is in love and not in hate the peoples have their actual being, their power to persist.

And so, since love cannot perish, neither can the peoples. The hate will die its death, and the darkness thereof dissolve, but the peoples will come forth anew. Their resurrection, divinely timed and glorious, is even now preparing. They may sleep long in the grave which the war has dug, and which the Conference of Paris has sealed. But whether it be soon, as history reckons time, or after searching sorrowful ages have come and gone, the peoples will rise again. They will rise at last, these now wrecked and woeful yet still warring nations, as one round communion of man, the kingdoms of the world become the kingdom of heaven, and the stains and the tears of history wiped away.

APPENDIX.

So if there exists an end for universal government among
men, that end will be the basic principle through which all things
to be proved hereafter may be demonstrated satisfactorily. But to
believe that there is an end for this government and for that
government, and that there is no single end common to all,
would indeed be irrational.

And since it is true that whatever modifies a part modifies the
whole, and that the individual man seated in quiet grows perfect
in knowledge and wisdom, it is plain that amid the calm and tran-
quility of peace the human race accomplishes most freely and
easily its given work. How nearly divine this function is revealed in the words, "Thou hast made him a little lower than the
angels." Whence it is manifest that universal peace is the best
of those things which are ordained for our beatitude. And hence
to the shepherds sounded from on high the message not of
riches, nor pleasures, nor honors, no length of life, nor health,
nor beauty; but the message of peace. For the heavenly host
said, "Glory to God in the highest, and on earth peace among
men in whom he is well pleased." Likewise, "Peace be unto you"
was the salutation of the Saviour of men. It befitted the supreme
Saviour to utter the supreme salutation. It is evident to all that
the disciples desired to preserve this custom; and Paul likewise in his words of greeting.

Dante in De Monarchia.

Further, a closer mutual approach of the States would essentially be demanded; a closer approach which in our days is more
than ever to be desired, in order to avert calamitous wars. What
the situation of Europe is we see with our own eyes. For
many years already we have had only an appearance of peace;
for mutual trust has disappeared, and made way for suspicion,
so that almost all the nations are vying with one another in arm-
ing themselves for war. Inexperienced youth will be cast into the
dangers of the military life, where it must dispense with the
counsel of its parents, and where their authority is withdrawn.
In the flower and vigour of their years the young men of the
world will be called to arms, and away from agriculture, from
beneficial studies, and from their trades or business pursuits.
Therefore, again, as a consequnce of the monstrous expenditure,
the State exchequer is drained, the wealth of the countries diminished, the individual property prejudiced. We have always
reached such a stage that armed peace has gradually become
unendurable. Can such a state of affairs be natural to civic
society?

Pope Leo XIII.

A LETTER TO THE PRESIDENT.

Le Retour,
Geneva, Switzerland,
May 31, 1918.

Dear Mr. President,

It is in obedience to the urgence, not only of authoritative individuals, but of whole peoples whom these individuals represent, that I take the liberty of addressing you on the subject of the immediate establishment of the Society of Nations.   Time after time, during the past quarter of a year, good and representative Europeans have urged me to cross the Atlantic and personally present to you their plea.   I could wish that yourself, with your singular political sensibilities, could for a brief time be in the midst of these peoples.   You would quickly understand, and no plea would be needed.

Not the lesser peoples alone are looking to you to speak soon the summoning word.   For this word our great Allies are even more anxiously waiting.   I do not mean their governments; for there is a daily widening mental cleavage between European governments and peoples.   It is by faith in what *America* will do,—it is above all by faith in what *you* will do,—and not by faith in governors and diplomats, that the nations are enduring the unimaginable strain and horror of this hour.   When I tell you that it is solely the faith of the peoples in *you,* in the word they are waiting for *you* to speak, that for now these many weeks has saved Europe from a condition akin to that of Russia, think not there is exaggeration or thought of personal compliment in what I say.   I am telling you the truth as radically, as nakedly, as mortal words can be made to tell it.   If anything is true, this is true—is sternly and divinely true: that this Continent would now be in a state of dissolution were it not for the hope of the peoples in *you*—in *your* championship of their liberties; in *your* shepherdship of the nationalities; in *your* commanding and creative call.   The peoples are trusting you to speak the word that shall gather them all into one fold, that shall form them into a federate world.

But the times grow perilous and imperative. The German penetration, its elusive and occult evil power,—more to be dreaded by far than the triumph of German arms,—this increases apace, despite all you may hear to the contrary; and the peoples grow evermore clamorous for you to formulate the purpose and the faith whereby they may endure the months if not years of sacrifice and sorrow now so terribly before them.

.   .   .   .

The peoples wish to know if you literally mean to establish the Society of Nations. If you do, send forth the summons now, they cry. With your spoken word before them as their pledge, as their uttered faith, as their "substance of the things hoped for," they are ready to endure the immeasurable tortures and griefs that may await them, that most probably do await them. They do not greatly trust either the wisdom or the integrity of their governments and governors: *they do trust you; they do trust America.* Already, your messages, the hope and the principles they expound, have become the very texture of the political mentality of European peoples. If you will make it to be that they war not only against the German dominion,—against the universal spiritual death that must issue from such dominion,—but they war for the creation of a new earth, then they are with you to the death. They will follow you as never mortal man was followed; nor will rulers or diplomats or financiers dare to say to them nay.

Not in the whole history of mankind, dear Mr. President, has the world turned to one man as it now turns to you. It is the supreme opportunity of mankind that stretches to you is appealing hands. So far as I can see,—so far as the infinitely wiser and better men than myself who have spoken to me can see,—no hand but yours can open the doors of this unprecedented and predestinative opportunity.

Will you open it? If you will, I believe the whole race of man will pass through that door, no matter what the travail and the tragedy of the passing, and that therethrough the race will enter upon a world of such fellowship and felicity, such new and nobler progress, as now seems incredible and Utopian.

I first spoke of France; but you will find the same response in England. The new Labor Party, as it is now organized, includes the best intellectual life of England, and the real English democracy. Such men as Professors Gilbert Murray and John G. Hobson (the greatest living political economist) are among its members. England is absolutely in the hands of this party. The British ruling-class exists only by the Labor Party's sufferance. Completely organized and splendidly poised, it only bides its time, concentrating its first energies upon the war against the German. The moment the war is ended, this party will take possession of England, and the British Empire will then become a wondrous and free confederation of nations. If you call for the Society of Nations to-day, this party and its leaders,— the best leaders that England has had for generations,— will be together with you.

Italy, too, will respond. Day before yesterday, I put the question to Marquis Paulucci, the Italian Minister here. "Would Italy give good answer?" I asked, "and would Baron Sonnino now respond favorably, if President Wilson should call for the Society of Nations?" His reply was instantly and earnestly in the affirmative.

The Serbians, the Czechs, the Poles, the Lettonians, and all the weaker peoples Germany has practically annexed,—all the uprising nationalities of the doomed and dissolving Hapsburg Empire,—would take your summons as their pledge of deliverance; they would hence proceed with such joyous assurance as would make their respective self-affirmations a power working vastly with the Allies for the overthrow of Germanism. The Czechs and Yougo-Slavs are already each a nearly-born nation, with their potential governments already formed and drilling. These wait only for your word. Once that is spoken, they will rise, and rise with noble effectiveness, against the seemingly triumphal German march.

Your summons would prove shattering to the Ger-
to the effect of a call from you for the establishment of

the Great Society. Such men as Professors Foerster and Jaffe of Munich; such as Herr Dr. Muehlon, the former Director-General of the Krupps works, whose exposure of German diplomacy have recently filled the world with amazement; such as Herr Konrad Hausmann, the acting Vice-chancellor, and Count Montgelas, who was formerly one of the ablest German commanders, —these are unanimous in their affirmation that your initiation of the Society of Nations would be the worst blow Germany could receive, and that delay of formation of this Society has been the greatest mistake of the Allies since the beginning of the war, or especially since America's entrance therupon.

Each of these authoritative men is of the opinion that even now such initiative on your part would do more to overthrow the power of the Prussian military class, of the dynasty also, than formidable military defeat. It would bring to the German peoples a feeling of guilt and shame that nothing else could produce. They would at last know themselves as outcast and pariah among nations. They would also see that, by establishment of the Society of Nations, their own just rights were secured, and that they had actually nothing to fight for except the perpetuity of their servitude to their masters. Your call would result in their first awakening from the Great Lie, the Great Delusion, the Great Hypnosis, under which they morally sleep while they yet physically put to shame the beasts of the jungle.

I have spoken of your immediate call for the Society of Nations as the only known anchor of common hope for the universal peoples. I have spoken of it as the shortest method of a moral conquest of Germany. I am also certain that it would prove to be a profound military tactic, a high and incomparable military strategy.

But there is now a more especial reason for the immediacy and urgency of this matter. It is the new peace offensive which Germany is preparing, and of which I am every day receiving information through German university friends. It is a peace offensive that will probably bring the nations to their most critical hour, and throw the whole responsibility for the yea or the nay as to the continuance of the war upon America,—upon you, Mr. President.

This will not be an offensive which begins by sending chosen messengers to such as myself, or by secret messages to Englishmen like Lord Lansdowne: it will be a peace offensive employing the mass tactic of the German military; it will be a vast and unexpected assault upon the whole moral front of the Allied peoples.

Germany will suddenly propose, especially if she is as measurably successful as I fear she will be in France, such apparently frank and generous terms to the Allies as will awaken a militant response in all the latent pacifist element, as well as among troubled and powerful financiers. She is seriously considering the question and the moment of offering Alsace-Lorraine to France, African colonies to England, independence and even restoration to Belgium, on condition that the territories east of the Rhine and the Adriatic shall not come into consideration at the Peace Conference. Let Germany have her way in the East; leave to her the future organization of Russia and Turkish territorties; then shall France and England and Belgium be given complete satisfaction, and even some concessions made to Italy and Serbia.

"Why sacrifice yourselves for Russia?" Germany will ask. "Why bleed yourselves white, why each of you commit national suicide, for the Russia that failed you utterly, and for territories and peoples with whom you have no near or real concern? We will organize them, giving them civil and economic capacity, creating markets for you as well as for ourselves. Our proved efficiency will take them out of barbarism and chaos, and put them on the road to government and progress. You will thus be free to develop your own special cultures anew. We make no claims upon you. We give you all you ask for yourselves. Let us now make peace, and together put the world in order. You are exhausting yourselves; and you see that we are unconquerable; especially as the East, with all its resources, now lies open to us."

There is to-day, as Germany knows, among the war-wearied peoples, a sentiment that would cry for the acceptance of these seemingly generous terms. The Allied nations are now partly mooded to respond favourably to such German appeal. For it would be an appeal, as I have already stated, not to individuals or to diplomats; it would be a public proclamation to the peoples.

What would result—supposing the Allied peoples even made such response as to paralyze partly the resisting power of their armies, and to give the Germans still further military advantage?

Germany would then have in hand the most compact and well-organized empire since the days of Rome at her greatest, and one more efficiently and tyrannically penetrated and ruled. Without interruption, the German Empire would stretch from the Rhine to the Pacific Ocean, so far as Northern Asia is concerned; and from Egypt to the gates of India, so far as the Near East is concerned, including inevitably all the present States of the Austro-Hungarian Monarchy, the control of the Mediterranean through Trieste and Salonika, and the lordship of the Bosphorous and the shores of Asia Minor. She would establish a swift economic penetration and dominion, taking away from the subject peoples all weapons of defence, all power or chance of military organizations, all economic freedom or initiative, forming them infallibly, without effectual resistance, according to the material and mental models of the essentially Satanic German "Kultur."

Furthermore, she is planning to make the peace proposals all the more appealing and effective by accompanying them with her own special plan for an organization of the Society of Nations. This is to be her great, her delectable suprise to the world. She thinks the surprise hidden in her diplomatic treasure house for the moment, but it will be no surprise to some of us who know. She expects to be able to say to the nations: "Behold! that which President Wilson and the Allies promised and did not, we now propose to do without having promised." And there are millions, alas! who will yield to the strong lie, to the Gargantuan delusion.

What, or who, can now save the peoples from a surrender to this double assault of an anti-Christ Germanism? What or who, can hold the peoples together through who knows what suffering, until America is ready with an effectual military leadership? What, or who, can stay the triumph of the German world-purpose when it masquerades in the terms of a broad and generous peace? What, or who, is sufficient to save mankind from the ages of iron darkness wherewith Germany is now more nearly overcoming the world than at any hour since she poured her well-nigh cosmical madness through Belgium's gates?

No one but yourself, Mr. President,—nothing but your own *immediate* summons of the nations to the sacred convocation that shall prepare their federation in a league for the compulsion of the world's just and permanent peace. No other than yourself can now speak the word that shall preserve the world from a German darkness and despotism infernal—the word, too, creating while it saves, that renders conscious the common but yet unuttered soul of mankind. No one but yourself is sufficient for proposing this world revolution, this new creation of the world:—a world wherein, when once it appears, men shall be no longer creatures but creators, choosing and directing the course of evolution, and writing hence the history of the future rather than of the past. No one but yourself can so speak to the present chaos as to compel the new creation's issue therefrom: no one but yourself is the recipient of the requisite universal confidence of mankind; no one but yourself is the possessor of an indisputable spiritual authority over the world.

You would wish to summon the best experts of America and the Allies to prepare the constitution of the Society. The details,—not so complicated and perplexing as they seem,—would have to be worked out. But you need not wait for these. Indeed, I make bold to say you dare not wait. You can boldly and broadly proclaim the Society's probable outline. You can arch forth, for the high quickening and resolute acceptance of the peoples, the commanding perspective.

Do this now; and the whole world, so helplessly driven hither and thither in one red wilderness of cynic confusion, will follow you as never Moses was followed by his tribes. Not the total course of human evolution, nor yet the stars in their courses, have committed unto man the shepherd's staff that now beseeches your hands.

I wish, Mr. President, I could put the power and immediacy of this appeal into words: I cannot. I wish there were words wherewith the appeal could be adequately and livingly stated: there are none. I wish you could know that it is no mere single individual who is speaking to you: that it is rather the long hope, so ancient yet perennial, that striveth and groaneth in the whole history and heartache of humanity. Yea, I dare say to you that it is the appeal of the immediate purpose of God in man to which you attend, as you consider these words, beset and baffled as they are with the writer's consciousness of their inadequacy and helplessness.

Let the League of Nations be now, Mr. President. Unto you it is divinely given, and unto you only, to speak the word that shall bring the World-Society into being. Not I, but all the shattered and sorrowing peoples entreat you to speak, and to speak while there is yet time.

Praying you pardon the presumption of this appeal, even while knowing as I do that it must be made, and remaining always your obedient and devoted servant, I am,

Faithfully yours,

GEORGE D. HERRON.

To His Excellency
Dr. Woodrow Wilson,
President of the United States of America,
Washington.

A TELEGRAM TO THE PRESIDENT

Le Retour, .
Geneva, Switzerland,
July 5, 1918.

Dear Mr. President,

My unhesitating and urgent answer to your crucial question is altogether affirmative.

In the course of a year, if the war continues, there will be no neutral nations. Both economic pressure and German intrigue will make neutrality impossible. Regardless of whether or not you now call for the Society of Nations, the nations still outside the conflict will be compelled to enter therein, choosing one camp or the other of the belligerents. The initiation of the Great Society by you, even if the neutrals delay to enter it, will place before them an almost unescapable motive for fighting side by side with America.

I cannot speak as to the present mind of all the neutrals. I do not know, for instance, the mental state of Sweden or of Spain. But I do know that, with the sacred sign of the Society of Nations before them, no earthly power could compel the Swiss people and their formidable army to fight upon the side of Germany. The same would be true of Norway; and I am of the opinion that your call would have a like effect upon Holland. In every case, the neutrals would be left without moral excuse for deciding against us.

Also, in each of these neutral countries, your proclamation would do more than all else to render powerless the malignant and penetrative German propaganda. And each of them, I believe, even if none of them at first dare accept the great invitation, would hail it with rejoicing. It is all to their interest to have the League formed: their self-preservation, the development of their respective national beings, absolutely depends upon the Society's formation. And even though they hesitated, for a time, to enter the new international regime, they would no less regard themselves morally as members thereof from the first.

Thus calling the Society into being, you will also complete America's ongoing spiritual conquest of Europe—by lifting the cause of America above reproach. And in lifting the cause of America above reproach, you will lift the whole cause of the Allies above reproach also. The peoples will then indeed believe the war against the Central Powers to be a war for the realization of a holy and liberating ideal.

Permit me also to say that if you propose reciprocal trade relations between the members of the Society you will by this one proposition destroy the chief cause of modern war. You will also undermine the fear of the German peoples—the fear so persistently cultivated by their masters—that if they sue for a peace that shall be acceptable to our Allies, these Allies will then take advantage of the surrender to encircle them with an impassible economic wall, making them virtual prisoners, for a long period of years, in an economic penitentiary. You would practically paralyze, by thus giving a moral basis to the commerce of Nations, the power of the German masters over the German people. Our moral conquest of even Germany would thus begin, rendering the military conquest less costly and more redemptive, saving a million or more young American lives by shortening the war. Indeed, I have reasons for knowing, as you will see by my dispatch sent yesterday through our Legation, that America's moral conquest of Germany is already beginning, and only needs this great word of yours to proceed apace.

May I make bold to urge you not to be influenced by the recent speeches in the British House of Lords? These men do not know the mind of Europe, nor even the mind of the English people. It is true, as the British lords contend, that the constitutional and juridical details of the Society will have to be worked out with care; but even so, the Society itself can be initiated, and its broad principles stated, without delay. If **we** long wait to summon the Society into being, if we continue to make caution our master, within a few months there may be no organized nations left in Europe to associate unto each other.

Of course, the governmental wise and the prudent will be against immediate action. But it is these wise and prudent ones who have brought the world to its present abysmal plight. Before the judgment bar of the present unimaginable crisis, the wisdom and the prudence of this world are an infidel and devastating foolishness.

I beg you not to hesitate, not to doubt. The destinies of mankind, for long centuries to come, depend upon your instant decision. To-morrow may be too late. You can to-day project before the nations the sign that will lift them out of an impasse that is already abysmal, and that is fast becoming literally infernal. You can expand our American Declaration of Independence into a declaration of the freedom and unity of humanity. You can speak the word that will pitch the whole course of history, the whole society of man, upon a new and comparatively divine plane of progress. You can wipe away the tears and the shames, the treasons and defeats, of two thousand years of universal disappointment.

In fine, Mr. President, by your immediate initiation of the Society of Nations, you will perform the most redemptive and creative act that has been performed for mankind since the paling lips of Him who initiated our Era pronounced His divine work finished.

Your devoted and obedient servant,

GEORGE D. HERRON.

To His Excellency,
Dr. Woodrow Wilson,
President of the United States of America,
Washington.

*THE WORLD SOCIETY INEVITABLE

I

Out of the swarm of evil things that came forth from Paris, two good things are discernable; the first of these negative but fundamental, the second positive and creative.

The first is the irrevocable manifestation of the misrepresentative character of all existing forms of government and diplomacy. The peoples of the planet Earth had about as little actual representation at the Conference of Paris as the peoples of the planet Mars. The logic of this manifestation is a complete democratic rebirth of all the institutions of social control, of national administration, and of international relations. Save by a democratic reconstruction of society, beginning with each communal group and widening out to include the world, we shall never have an associative or peaceful world, a true society of nations.

The second good escape from Paris is the idea of the Society of Nations. The present proposed League of Nations is, as I have already explained or protested, only such in name. It is in fact a league of governments, in no sense a league of nations; and it is also a league for the coercion of the peoples in the interests of an international capitalism, and not a league of peoples for their own peace and freedom. As it is now constructed, it has no value to the peoples; and, if it becomes operative, will constitute only a power for the suppression of the peoples and the thwarting of their aspirations.

But the idea contained in the League is so infinitely greater and more living than the League itself that there is no possibility that the frame-work of this League can endure; and there is the largest mortal certainty that the idea will endure and construct for itself, ultimately, a true and living body. And that living body will be a literal world-state or world-society, fulfilling Tennyson's prophecy of the parliament of man, the federation of the world.

---

* Published in *The League of Nations*, Bern, February 10th, 1920.

Let it be remembered that President Wilson himself regarded the present League of Nations only as a temporary embodiment of the living idea—as the best that could be had to begin with—and that he expected that the idea would effectuate itself in an appropriate form in due time, once it were accepted by the nations.

II

Now it is profoundly important that we consider immediately, yet with due deliberation, the principles and processes by which a real democratic society of nations can be brought into being, either as a development of the present provisional League or as a growth alongside that League. It may, and probably will be, that the events of the next two or three years, of the next few months indeed, will render most of our discussions superfluous. The divinity that resides even in the worst events will have scrapped most of our programs and many of our problems. Yet these discussions will have served their purpose. They will keep the idea of a society of nations, embracing all peoples within its fold, constantly and germinatively in the thought of these peoples. And to fix the idea of the world as one society of kindred peoples is the first and most vital thing to be done. We must see to it that surely, and as quickly as possible, the peoples realize that they are one family of men, and that divisions between them are always the work of the Appetites and Interests that prey upon them.

Every influence that arrays one people against another people is predatory and parasitic. The dividers of men are by the same token the blasphemers of God. For not only is it the basic truth of all the prophets, all the religions, that we are members one of another: it is the basic lie, the basic blasphemy, the basic diabolism, that teaches us that we are enemies one of another and that the interests of one human group conflict with the interests of another human group. These conflicts of interest exist, it is true, but they have not grown out of any actual or spiritual law: they are the creations of the Appetites and Interests and Powers that exist by and fatten upon these conflicts.

This is why a League of Nations (such as the present league) that presumes to impose peace *upon* the peoples, is an impudence. It is not the peoples who make wars; it is not the peoples who break the peace; it is not the peoples who need to have peace imposed upon them. It it the governments that make wars; it is the hireling press of the Appetites that cultivates the hatreds between peoples and precipitates the conflicts. And thus the first step towards a Society of Nations is in the direction of the complete democratization of the present League, or else the creation of a democratic League to take place of the one coming out of Paris.

III

But, before this can be done, the governments themselves must be democratized.

There exists no such thing as a democratic government or democratic state. All existing governments are essentially oligarchic in character and administration. We cannot have a democratic League of Nations if none of the nations are democratically constituted. And none of them are.

Thus the league of the peoples must be the work of the peoples. It is hopeless to expect delegates appointed by existing governments to formulate a democratic League of Nations. The delegates who shall formulate such a league must be sent directly and proportionately by the several peoples themselves. They must not even be elected by parliaments, as parliaments are now constituted; for these, though nominally elected by the peoples are almost universally appointed, behind the scenes, by the Interests and Appetites. The delegates of a democratic league must be elected by the direct popular and secret vote of the peoples.

The best immediate preparation for such a realization would be a continuance of the work begun in Brussels. The different peace societies of the world, assembling as they did at Brussels, should establish immediately a free and open international parliament, a parliament which should be in continuous session and deliberation and discussion, and should establish its own executive headquarters at Geneva. This would either evolve into the real Society of Nations itself, and consequently would duly supplant the coercive League of Governments that issued from the Paris conference, or else it would compel this League to submit itself to being created anew by the representatives of the peoples.

But this parliament should invite and welcome every shade of opinion to its forum. It should not only ask all the socialist parties to speak their minds, through chosen representatives: it should not only ask Lenin to send from Moscow someone who would truly speak his mind: it should also ask the Pope to send from the Vatican a representative who would state the idea of the Catholic Church concerning the Society of Nations. It should aim, this parliament I plead for, to be a real forum of man and of every kind of human opinion concerning the organization of the world. Only so, by universal invocation and tolerance, by getting every kind of opinion about the organization of the world frely and fully expressed, could an accordant world at last become a possibility.

IV

Furthermore, only so can the first basis of a real Society of Nations be established—namely, the trust of the peoples in the peoples.

If the Son of Man should come to-day, not only would he fail to find any real faith in himself as a practical organizer of human life: he would fail to find faith of any kind: he would fail to find one people which trusts another people: I am not sure that he would find a man who trusts another man.

And when all is said and done about Paris, I am afraid it will be found that its most characteristic work—and a very evil work indeed—has been the destruction of what little faith formerly did exist in the world between nations and between groups of men.

Who trusts the peoples? Certainly no government trusts the particular people it governs. Lenin does not trust the Russian people. He knows perfectly well that the Russian peasants will not go his way except by coercion. Clemenceau knows the same thing regarding the French people. There is absolutely no moral difference between Clemenceau's and Lenin's respective conceptions of control. Neither of them trusts his people; and each of them merely camouflages his faith in despotism, and in despotism only. The British Imperial Government will risk nothing in the way of democracy in Ireland or Egypt or India. American plutocracy will risk nothing in the way of free expression of public opinion in America. In fact, all power of whatever sort, is to-day built upon unfaith in the peoples and upon an exploitive infidelity to their interests. Hence the beginning of a democratic society of nations must be in a release of the mind of the peoples, and of the minds and methods of those who really represent them. It is only faith in the peoples, leaving them free to express themselves and free to act, that will remove the mountainous difficulties in the way of international peace and international administration.

V

But the basis of a democratic league will not be military nor even political: it will be economic and social. It will concern itself with the real concerns of the peoples.

And an International Tribunal must be created, in order to make any Society of Nations effective; and it must be a Tribunal to which all members of the League or Society agree to submit their difficulties and problems for final arbitrage.

But just because its decisions are final, the Tribunal must be as representative of the peoples as the international parliament itself. I know that there will immediately arise the old jargon about the needs of specialists in international law and all that. The peoples, it will be said, will have no knowledge of who is wisest in these matters. But this jargon concerns one of the fetishes, one of the ancient superstitions, that will have to be got rid of. What is needed in the world to-day is social wisdom rather than technical legal knowledge.

Our old American poet who said that "it is the heart and not the brain that to the highest doth attain," spoke with Christly wisdom.

The one place in this world from which wisdom is farthest, where indeed wisdom casts no shadow, is in the existing governing classes and bodies. I would a hundred times over trust the social wisdom of a group of unlettered Russian peasants before I would trust any knowledge or wisdom supposed to reside in the French Chamber of Deputies or the American House of Congress. If these two bodies are not the incarnation of all the ignorance of history concerning the real thought and feeling of the peoples, I do not know where to look for such ignorance.

The old Saxon Wittenagemote and the early Swiss Landesgemeinde are the microcosm of what the universal microcosm must be. The faith of the peoples in the peoples is the beginning of the wisdom, of the only wisdom, that can federate the world in one body of organic and administrative goodwill.

*ABOUT PRINKIPO.

Le Retour,
Geneva,
Switzerland.
Oct. 1st, 1919.

Editor of *The New Republic*.
New York City.

Sir,

In your issue of August 27th, in an editorial article entitled, "More Light on Open Diplomacy," I find statements so precisely the opposite of facts about the Prinkipo affair that I think they should be corrected.

In the first place (though of incidental concern) you are mistaken in your attribution of the proposal to an American origin. Prinkipo was a British proposal— a proposal afterwards abandoned in a panic, as should have been expected, by its eminently reponsible proposer.

In the next place—and this is what is important—the proposal was *not* finally rejected by the anti-bolshevist parties and governments of Russia. From the moment that I was asked to go to Prinkipo I labored to persuade all Russian parties to participate in the conference. My chief argument was, that no intelligent or justifiable action could be taken regarding Russia—at least by America—until all Russian factions had been fully heard, both by each other and the Allies, in free and open meeting. The chief of what remained of the Cadets, and certain personal followers of Miliukov, met me at Geneva, as did also a representative of the Omsk Government. These finally agreed, after repeated representations on my part, to come to Prinkipo. In Paris, I discussed the plan with other Russian representatives, especially with the revered and venerable **Tchaikovsky**. On different occasions Tchaikovsky met with Mr. White and myself, and with numerous other persons interested in the question of what to do with Russia. He at last agreed to put no more obstructions in the way of the Prinkipo plan, and indeed bcame very helpful to Mr. White and myself in making suggestions as to our course of action. This concession on the part of Tchaikovsky was due largely to the influence of Mr. Gompers and Mr. English Walling, who also rendered Mr. White and my-

---

* Published in the *New Republic* of December 3rd, 1919.

self valuable assistance in conferring with other Russians in Paris. It finally came about that, with the exception of Sazonov, who really represented French finance and the Romanoffs, every considerable Russian party or government had come round to the Prinkipo proposal, and expected to participate in the projected conference. And then, behind the back of Mr. White and myself, and of the regularly appointed representatives of Great Britain and France and Italy, Mr. Bullitt and his colleagues were sent to Lenin and Trotsky. When we asked Hotel Crillon for information about this mission—which was the very quintessence of secret diplomacy—and which was also typical of that senseless lack of candor, that juvenile calculativeness, that childish egotism, which particularly characterized our proceedings in Paris, and which had the effect of preventing the President (though he is never likely to know or believe it) from at any time perceiving what was really going on—we were met only with denial and evasion. Mr. Bullitt himself, the very hour in which he was on his way to the Embassy to arrange his passports, unaware that I knew he was starting to Moscow, vehemently assured me as to his fidelity to Prinkipo.

Previous to this, however, when Mr. White and myself were daily expecting to proceed about the fulfilment of our appointment, we made two explicit demands:

1. That we must be allowed to go without any entangling instructions. We must be free to make our own investigations in our own way and to arrive at our own conclusions.

2. That all meetings between ourselves and the Russians must be public. We meant to meet in the market-place. We would have to do with no secret conferences, no subterranean arrangements. Every accredited journalist, every worthy citizen of any country, who wished to be present and hear all that was said, should be admitted. In the completest sense of the word, whatever took place was to be of the nature of an unqualified open diplomacy.

Now it was just when the consent of all Russian parties to participate had been obtained, with the one exception mentioned, that the mission of Mr. Bullitt was dispatched. I then undertook to explain to the American Commissioner who had the Russian matter in hand that we were now especially responsible for our action in this Russian matter, all the Russians having accepted the Prinkipo proposition. But the Commissioner in question suddenly decided that he would not hear more of Russia until he had further information as to what England would do. Two days afterwards, without any explanation whatever concerning the reasons for the decision, and without any further opportunity of conferring with the Peace Commissioners, with whom I had been in conference about other matters, Mr White and myself were unceremoniously informed by the chief clerk of the American Commission—summoned to his presence by one of his clerks—that the Prinkipo proposition was dropped.

Now what I want to make clear is this: that so far as Hotel Crillon was concerned, the general movement and tendency was in favor of recognising the government of Lenin and Trotsky. I heard a good many voices in and around that unhappy hunting-ground, while the question of Prinkipo was held in the balance, and all the voices were in favor of an agreement with the Soviet Government, and not one voice was against it. I am not debating whether this was a correct policy or not: I am merely stating the fact. In the next place, it was only when it was discovered that *all* Russian parties *were* likely to participate in the Conference, and that the Conference would be open to the world, that Prinkipo lost favor with Hotel Crillon.

Let me conclude by absolving Mr. White of all knowledge of and responsibility for this letter, and at the same time pay my tribute to his unfailing unselfishness, to the chivalry and kindliness of his co-operation, in the days when we were preparing for what we hoped would prove a pivotal service to America, to Russia and to the world.

GEORGE D. HERRON.

AGAINST THE RUSSIAN BLOCKADE.

Le Retour,
Geneva,
Switzerland.
Oct. 23, 1919.

Editor of *Times,*
  New York City.

Sir,

As one who is not a bolshevist but very much the contrary, but who yet believes in the principle of self-determination as applied to nationalities, I wish to register my protest, however impotent, it may be, against the essential military alliance of Great Britain, France and Germany, coupled with the moral alliance of America, for the invasion of Russia. Especially do I wish to give voice to the general horror of the peoples international at the intensification of the blockade against Russia; which blockade must inevitably result in the death of a large part of the Russian child population.

And indeed what a spectacle is this—the alliance of three Great Powers with their recent enemy—with the Power they pronounced the enemy of mankind in fact—in order that, by making war upon millions of children and their mothers, they may insure the payment of the Czarist debts and secretly restore the Romanoffs to the imperial throne. It is only the callousness produced by the horrors of five years of war, and produced also by the still greater horrors proceding from the Peace of Paris, that prevents the whole of mankind from rising in burning indignation against this unholy alliance and its motives and operations. The cruelties of Nero, or of the ancient Oriental monarchs, are but nursery plays as compared with this alliance of ours and the Entente with Germany for the extermination by starvation of the childhood of a vast and fallen empire—in the interests of international moneylenders.

Was it for this that the young men of our great Middle-West were called to France—on a "holy war," on a "crusade" against Germanism and for democracy? Is this black thing the democracy we were asked to make the world safe for? I use the word black advisedly: for when the history of the future comes to be written, and written in the light of the principles for which we professed to make war, this intensified blockade against Russia in her agony, this alliance with Germany for the destruction of democratic opportunity and the re-enthronement of the Romanoffs, will surely be set down as a foul cruelty, as a black betrayal. I am certain that if the American people knew what was thus being done, they would wash their hands clean of this alliance straightway and forever. Moreover, if the Entente and America wish to render certain a bolshevist revolution and régime throughout the world, they are choosing the precise means of accomplishing just such an end.

I say this, also, not only as one who has again and again warned those who sit in America's high places against the bolshevist movement: I speak as one who advocates America's responsibility for the world. I believe it is better for mankind, better for the soul of America, that we accept mandates for the peoples who seek our protection. I would place Armenia, Constantinople, Macedonia, and Albania all under American protection and administration. But what we are doing in Russia is a contradiction of all this. It is the essential refusal of our world-burden. We are intervening, at least tacitly and morally, in aid of an unimaginably base betrayal and butchery of a people who are struggling, through terrible experiences, to find a national life and self-expression that shall be indigenously their own.

Faithfully yours,

GEORGE D. HERRON.

*IN ANSWER TO A GERMAN ACCUSER

MERAN,
ALTO ADIGE,
ITALY.
DEC. 8th, 1921.

DEAR MR. SCHEFFAUR,

I can easily understand your taking amiss my failure to write to you after your courteous "Open Letter." My apology is the complete breakdown of my health, against which I have been struggling for more than a year, and which gave me many weeks in bed, and which is now causing my banishment from Geneva to the mountains, and to the undergoing of a long cure for the winter. Almost everything has been neglected by the force of circumstances, and all promised work had to be given up.

I can therefore write only briefly in reply to your word, which has just come, and which I am sure you would not have written if you knew the actual facts of my labor during the War and the Peace Conference.

There is absolutely no mystery or secrecy about what I tried to do. I thought my book and other articles had made the matter entirely clear. Let me put the matter into three or four brief statements.

I. It is true that I believed Germany guilty of precipitating the war, and that I used all such small influence as I had toward getting America into the war on the side of the Entente. I did this under the compelte faith, however naive that faith may now seem, that America would transmute the whole motivity and result of the war, would indeed make it a war to end war, and would hence see to it that no vindictive measures should be taken toward Germany, even while seeing to it that justice was exacted for what Germany had done to Belgium, to France and to the world.

II. It is true that I believed absolutely in Wilson's program, from beginning to end; that I believed equally in his personal integrity in the matter; that I believed

---

*Published in the *Berlin Herald,* April 15th, 1922.

in his entire ability to carry through his program. And upon all except Wilson's ability to carry through his program, my faith is just as fixed now as it was then. Wilson's program would have given us a new and vastly better international order, if it had been carried out. Wilson was perfectly honest in his intentions to have it carried out. He was duped and defeated by the makers of the monstrous Peace of Versailles.

III. It is true that I did my utmost to persuade the German missions that came to me during the war to put their faith in Wilson and his program. I did my utmost, in all good faith, to undermine German resistance, confident in my own mind that if Germany would cease fighting and appeal to Wilson, the war would end in a great moral victory. I also did my utmost to persuade these German missions as to the moral as well as political value of making a confession of Germany's guilt in beginning the war. I then believed this would be good for Germany, and I believed it would be a way to prevent a peace of revenge.

IV. It is true that I urged the Munich Government, at the head of which was Kurt Eisner, to take such an initiative. But the beginning of this matter was with Eisner and his government, and not with me. The day they took over the Bavarian Government, Eisner and two of his ministers telegraphed me at length requesting my intervention on their behalf with President Wilson. I believed at the time that if some encouragement from the President were practicable or possible, the government of Eisner could lay the foundation for a new and democratic Germany that would perhaps compensate to some measure for the horrors of the war. I did my utmost, but failed.

Now certainly it is true that everything that I labored for during the War, and the time of the making of the Peace, has turned into disastrous and apparently unqualified failure. The Peace of Versailles, and the whole course of the Entente, especially of France, since the prolongation of the Peace, has been an explicit violation of the solemn compact made with Germany by the signing of the Armistice, and has been bearing the whole world toward the abyss, if not to a new series of Dark Ages. It is true that I made promises to the German missions that came to me—and for that matter to peoples all over these three continents of the Old World—that were never kept. But I made those promises in absolute good faith. I believed in them, with every atom of my being, in every accent and syllable of them. I had nothing to gain by my labors: the world had nothing I wanted— except the opportunity, or what I then thought was the opportunity, to help mankind into a new order of collective being—an order that should be a real approach to the kingdom of heaven. That those promises have not been kept is not the moral fault of President Wilson. Nor is it because I, in my small way, failed to work for their fulfilment. And it does not help Germany, it only does Germany harm, for you so violently to impugn the honesty of men who have themselves been betrayed by the Great Betrayal, and who have been broken on the wheel by the Powers that wrought that Betrayal. You do not help Germany by adding to the awful cup of the world's bitterness. And all this, however absurd or pitiful my faith has since proved itself to have been, however mistaken its premises.

In conclusion, let me say that, since the Peace of Versailles, no one has denounced that Peace more than I. No one has pointed out our perjury toward Germany more than I. No one has condemned the makers of that treaty more than I. No one has fought more unremittingly and unqualifiedly for justice and mercy toward Germany than I. And I have fought alone many times, with my back to the wall, bereft of all influence, and knowing even as I fought that I would fail. And I have had to fight, assailed by the malediction of such Americans as you on the German side and by the equally violent maledictions of the French press on the other side, while upon my head rest the curses of the organs and agents of the international financiers who brought about the Great War in the beginning, who brought about the Peace of Versailles, and who are today bringing about the death of civilization in the hope of feasting on civilization's dead body.

All this is by the way of personal explanation which I hope will carry with it some appeal to your understanding. Of course, what happens to me is a matter of no importance whatever, and it is with no such thought that I write. It is only what is happening to humanity that matters. But I write in the hope of dissolving some of the bitterness and the misjudgments of which you are perhaps all unwittingly making yourself guilty, and which misjudgments can only add to the woe of the world.

Faithfully yours,

GEORGE D. HERRON.

Mr. Hermann George Scheffauer,
Cuno Strasse 48,
Berlin-Grunewald.